OBSERVING LEARNING IN EARLY CHILDHOOD

STELLA LOUIS

OBSERVING LEARNING IN EARLY CHILDHOOD

Los Angeles | London | New Delhi
Singapore | Washington DC | Melbourne

Los Angeles | London | New Delhi
Singapore | Washington DC | Melbourne

SAGE Publications Ltd
1 Oliver's Yard
55 City Road
London EC1Y 1SP

SAGE Publications Inc.
2455 Teller Road
Thousand Oaks, California 91320

SAGE Publications India Pvt Ltd
B 1/I 1 Mohan Cooperative Industrial Area
Mathura Road
New Delhi 110 044

SAGE Publications Asia-Pacific Pte Ltd
3 Church Street
#10-04 Samsung Hub
Singapore 049483

Acquisitions editor: Delayna Spencer
Assistant editor: Bali Birch-Lee
Production editor: Zoheb Khan
Copyeditor: Clare Weaver
Proofreader: Derek Markham
Indexer: KnowledgeWorks Global Ltd.
Cover design: Wendy Scott
Typeset by: KnowledgeWorks Global Ltd.
Printed in the UK

Library of Congress Control Number: 2022939612

British Library Cataloguing in Publication data

A catalogue record for this book is available from the British Library

ISBN 978-1-5297-6780-3
ISBN 978-1-5297-6779-7 (pbk)

At SAGE we take sustainability seriously. Most of our products are printed in the UK using FSC papers and boards. When we print overseas we ensure sustainable papers are used as measured by the PREPS grading system. We undertake an annual audit to monitor our sustainability.

For my daughter Hannah, her husband Adam, Puds, and Bailey with love,
March 2022

CONTENTS

ABOUT THE AUTHOR

Dr Stella Louis is a freelance Early Years consultant. She originally trained as a NNEB nursery nurse and has taught on the NNEB specialising in observations. Stella has thirty-four years' experience of working with children and families. For the last ten years she has been involved in training educators and is particularly interested in observation and its part in supporting learning, development and teaching. Currently, Stella leads a small team of Froebelian travelling tutors in promoting, developing and delivering the Froebel Trust Short Courses in the United Kingdom.

Stella is author of numerous books and articles including *Observing Young Children* (SAGE), *Understanding Schemas in Young Children* (Bloomsbury) and *How to use Group Supervision to Improve Early Years Practice* (Routledge).

Stella has worked both in the United Kingdom and internationally, in South Africa, where she worked with teachers to develop a Froebelian approach to teaching and learning. For the last eight years Stella has been the lead trainer in a project led by Professor Tina Bruce in Kliptown, Soweto, South Africa. Stella has extensive experience working with children and their families in England, South Africa and Australia.

ACKNOWLEDGEMENTS

I would like to thank the following people for permission to use observations – Kate Razzal, Tina Bruce and Carol Bromley and team. I would also like to acknowledge Stephaine Harding, for our useful discusions and reflections on each chapter.

1
WHY OBSERVATIONS MATTER

Introduction

By unpicking the process, this chapter aims to examine why observations matter. It will look extensively at how observations can be used as a tool and an integral part of daily practice. Observation pedagogy matters and this book will be a reflective tool to help Early Childhood Education (ECE) students evaluate and reflect on observations. It will also act as a resource for considering the ways in which different settings undertake and use observations to inform teaching and learning by noticing, recognising, responding and reflecting.

There is a longstanding tradition of observation within Early Childhood settings, which contributes to our understanding of how children develop and learn (Froebel, 1887; Isaacs, 1929). Isaacs recognised the importance of observation, noting,

> It cannot, of course, be very easy for us to gain a clear idea of what the world is like to a very young child, just because it must be so different from our own. But by patient listening to the talk of even little children, and watching what they do, with the one purpose of understanding them, we can imaginatively feel their fears and angers, their bewilderments and triumphs; we can wish their wishes, see their pictures and think their thoughts. (1929: 15)

These observations focus on looking at, listening to and recognising what a child does. They focus on what a child is intrigued by, or is inquiring about, as well as describing and supporting the way a child approaches learning. Ongoing observation is a vital part of the teaching and learning process.

Observations are used to get to know babies, toddlers and young children well. ECE students will be required to observe children on a regular basis, identifying their stages of development, interests and ways of learning. An important premise which underpins the practice of observation is that ECE students should be knowledgeable about what a typical child's development looks like. This will help them to see relevant learning so that they can match this with the stage of development and learning that a child has reached. Observing children effectively requires ECE students to combine different types of knowledge about the stages and processes of development and learning. This includes not just knowledge of child development but also of how children think, feel and learn through play.

Why Observations are Important

Let's begin with the question of why observations are important to one's practice.

Observation helps ECE students to understand a child's needs and interests and how they learn best. An observation is like a story about the child and what they are doing. It captures a moment in time that tries to understand and interpret their knowledge, behaviour and what they need. The role of the observer is not an easy one. They need to be patient, self-controlled and have a great deal of awareness, knowledge and understanding about typical development. They must see the implications of the children's actions, remarks and questions and act on or respond to them immediately. They need to keep ongoing records of the significant things that children do, note down what they say, and then reflect on the meaning of the child's actions or words, as well as knowing how to support or extend them. As a general rule, observations should always include the date, the context in which learning is taking place, and should describe a child's significant thinking, development and learning. They also need the time and the name of the observer.

Observing and Recognising Children's Learning

These kinds of observations are important because they not only seek to meet children's unique and diverse needs but also help us to review how appropriate our provision for them is. Our observations of children give us a picture of their actions, behaviour or focus and they can be used to help us figure out where the child could be with help and support. It's only through observing children that we learn about them, what they can do, and what they need help with or are interested in. If ECE students know what a child can do, they can then use this information to facilitate, support and extend their learning. This aspect of observation practice is vital. It requires ECE students to know not only what a child can do, but also how to take the child to the next level of learning (Vygotsky, 1978).

With knowledge of child development – and understanding gained from ongoing observations of children's learning – we will know when we need to provide the child with more of the same kinds of experiences, while tracking their progress and understanding their hopes, desires and fears. In this sense, observation ensures that we are also better able to plan to meet their individual needs. Without observing young children, planning by ECE students would be based on assumptions about what is appropriate, using their own knowledge and experience. The more ECE students know about what interests, motivates and engages a child, the more appropriately they will be able to support learning.

The Process of Observation

The slow, reflective and analytical process of observing babies, toddlers and young children is important – it enables us to consider the finer detail and make connections with child development theories. That said, observing children's active learning is not a simple task. Noticing children demonstrate a particular skill and interpreting the implications of their actions can be complex and difficult work (Nutbrown and Carter, 2010). It is challenging to work out what children are thinking while observing them in a variety of different situations, as well as interpreting and understanding the child's stage of development and experience and recording achievements as we support them in their development and learning. Observing children's interests is about more than just watching – it involves studying detail and patterns repeated across the child's play, considering their first-hand experience and their cultural background while linking this with what is known about child development, what the child can do and what the child is interested in. Bringing together this vital information enables us to know what to expect from individual children and it is critical to observe them in different contexts to ensure that assessments are fair. Ultimately, our observations help us to understand our children and effectively provide them with experiences that build on their interests. Unless we take time to observe babies, toddlers and young children – and understand what we see – we cannot help them very much (Bartholomew and Bruce, 1993).

When we reflect on our observations, we understand what may be inhibiting children's development and/or learning. We can then make the necessary changes to the environment that enable children to overcome this challenge, all the time building on what they know and can do. Observation is more than just teaching – it becomes an integral part of ECE students' everyday work. Effective observation, if done well, creates the conditions for successful development and learning. That's why it is important.

Observation Training Matters

Carrying out observations is a skill that needs to be learned. This skill will become developed and refined with regular practice. Developing skill in observations is not a sprint, but a marathon – training in observation will be ongoing and prepares ECE students for professional practice. It involves learning how to observe, listen and think objectively about what children have been seen doing. In practice, this means drawing on knowledge of child development, not allowing preconceptions to influence what has been observed, and striving to make sense of what has been seen. ECE students will be expected to make a judgement about what has been observed as well as deciding how they might further support or extend the child's learning.

Developing Observation Pedagogy

Observation pedagogy concerns how we think about children as individuals when we design our teaching programme, invent activities, and prepare purposeful learning experiences that will link to and reinforce children's previous experiences. In this way, we show our understanding of the different stages of development a child goes through; each stage dependent on what has gone before. It includes how we accommodate each stage of development as needing to be experienced fully and not rushed. It also involves how carefully we watch and listen to what a child says and does, how we think about the child's needs in the context of our teaching, how we interact with children and our relationships with them, and the ability to ask the child meaningful questions and listen to their responses.

Developing observation pedagogy is central to our teaching practice as observation is the main tool that ECE students use to come to an understanding about children's learning. Without observations as the bedrock of practice we cannot effectively focus our teaching on the individual child. Observation is an important tool in effective teaching and learning because it gives ECE students a starting point when considering where the child is in their learning and understanding. Although children go through specific stages of development, the stages are not fixed and are dependent upon experience. According to Froebel (1887), students must be aware of these different developmental stages and he urges them to consider whatever stage the child is at.

Young children do not learn only when they are instructed by others. They learn through purposeful play activities, with educators who understand how best to guide them. As such, the activities and experiences that we offer children need to be based on what we have learned from our observations of them. Good teaching is a vital ingredient in progression and ensures that all children experience meaningful learning opportunities across all areas of development.

Although it is not possible to observe absolutely everything that a child does, we can focus our observations on capturing significant learning. If our observations are to be of importance they need to influence the child's immediate learning situation. Observation, assessment and planning are part of an interrelated cycle which we will discuss further in Chapter 2. Sometimes we need to respond to the child in the moment – we might need to stand back or encourage them by offering help. How we respond will depend on the child and our relationship with them as some children are extroverts, other children are introverted, some children are confident, others are not. It is also important to be aware of how your presence may change play – it may make children feel more secure or it may make them more inhibited.

The ongoing development of observation practice implies a pedagogy in which ECE students are both engaged and aware of how they effectively support and extend children's individual development and learning. Observation skills are not simply developed by watching children – they come about when we take action to offer the child what they need for their further development, leading to new insight about that child. Unless our planning is based on systematic observations of young children, we may unwittingly expect them to learn through a fixed and inflexible curriculum. Observations help us to fit the curriculum around children's individual needs, rather than expecting children to fit into the curriculum.

Observation As a Tool

Observing the rapid changes as a child develops and unfolds is fascinating. Changes and growth take place in all areas of development – physical, mental, language, social and emotional – and these areas overlap and influence each other. As a result, ECE students will be expected to regularly observe changes in babies, toddlers and young children in order to build up a holistic picture of their growth and progression. These observations need to capture and describe how children engage and interact thoughtfully in play and explorations.

Babies, toddlers and young children learn through their interactions with people, objects and situations as well as their first-hand experiences and encounters with the world. They will use these experiences to help them to navigate their way through life. Playing and exploring is the natural way in which young children learn and ECE students will observe children becoming involved as they struggle with new experiences through manipulation and discovery. These experiences help young children to practise, remember and incubate their thoughts and ideas as they begin to link them with previous experiences. ECE students will be expected to observe what intrigues or motivates children, how they discover things for themselves, or how deeply involved and engaged they are while playing pretend games. Tuning into how children test out their own ideas or solve problems will reveal information about their interests. ECE students will also be expected to observe how children make sense of the world around them, how they develop the content of their ideas, and how they take charge of their own learning. ECE students need to understand children's thinking, so that they can help them to make connections and apply their existing knowledge to new situations in meaningful ways.

Observation Methods

How ECE students carry out systematic observations of a child's development and record their learning will depend on several factors. These include the individual skill of the observer, knowledge of typical development, and the setting in which they work. Some settings use a digital platform or Tablet for observing and recording while others use photographs with a brief description or Sticky notes. An example may be taking a series of three photographs of a child's development over a two-week period. The first photo captures the child's attempt to climb over a large log. The second, taken a few days later, shows that the child is able to climb further. The third reveals that the child is able to climb across the log by the end of the second week. These sequenced and systematic photos illustrate the process of learning, making it possible to obtain relevant information about fundamental aspects of the child's development. A single photograph at the end of the process may demonstrate that the child can climb but it will tell us little about their actions or focus. It is therefore fundamental that ECE students consider the systems of knowledge under which photographs of children learning are interpreted and analysed (Flannery Quinn and Manning, 2013). ECE students are advised to use a variety of methods, such as discussions with the children, questioning, planned and spontaneous observations, professional dialogue and parents' observations from home.

Parents As Partners and As Observers

ECE students have an important role to play in supporting parents, particularly new parents, to understand their child's drive to learn. Babies, toddlers and young children may not yet have the words to express their needs, ideas and feelings. However, parents can usually interpret these cues in their child's behaviour and will know how they are feeling or what they may want (Whalley, 2017). This is ultimately what partnerships with parents is about – working together to develop real meaningful understanding about individual children's development and disposition to learn.

Students need to see parents as active observers of their child's development and use parental observations as a means of establishing partnerships with them. Students can encourage parents to observe, interact and participate in their child's play, sometimes supporting and extending it alongside the child. Encouraging parents to share their observations of learning at home can be revealing about how parents value their children's play. When students work with parents in this way, they develop strong partnerships with them based on respect and understanding.

For example, a parent shared the following observation with an ECE student – Raphael (2 years, 5 months) put five toy cars on the seat of his pushchair and went behind to push it, saying 'my babies' and then 'mine mummy'. His parent explained to the student that 'mine mummy' meant 'I am mummy' and 'my babies' is his brother, as he was not secure on pronouns. Raphael's parent was fascinated by this particular observation when the ECE student shared her thoughts with them – that this was Raphael's way of learning, using the cars and the pushchair symbolically to express his knowledge of the way in which he was nurtured by his family and his understanding that he too can be nurturing. It is clear from this example that the parent and the student understood the observation differently, yet both made valued interpretations. It is important to point out that parents and ECE students will interpret observations of children's play and explorations according to their own expectations, knowledge and beliefs. Effective partnerships are based on having meaningful two-way conversations, acknowledging, listening to and valuing parents' concerns about their child's development and, at the same time, respecting each other's viewpoint and supporting parents to attain the best early education for their child.

Observing Children's Differences

Every child has their own unique and diverse ways of approaching learning and we must keep in mind that children learn at their own pace and in their own way. To help each child according to their own needs, interests and ways of learning, ECE students need to know as much as possible about them. For example, while all children are active learners, some children may be interested in observing the things around them in thoughtful ways. Others may want to explore and investigate things, play pretend games, build with blocks or use symbols to represent their experiences in imaginative and abstract ways. ECE students will be expected to know whether a child might need more of the same or if the play needs to be extended by expanding the learning. When ECE students observe children they need to consider and be aware of their differences.

Some children may come from a different culture and have the setting country's language as an additional one. Other children may experience specific barriers to learning. ECE students need to be aware of how these differences may affect children and not make assumptions about their actions and behaviours.

As we begin to observe children, listen to what they say, and engage with them, we discover not only their interests but also how they approach learning. It is from this point that ECE students begin to make judgements about how children prefer to learn.

Observing children's interests presents a number of challenges because young children pass through specific stages of learning where they are more interested in watching, seeking, finding, feeling and investigating. The process of what the child is doing is important. It cannot be assumed that babies, toddlers and young children learn every time they are provided with an activity or experience. ECE students can facilitate learning by observing and supporting children based on what they need now and thinking about how to better match the environment with what the child needs to progress. How they make judgements about children's learning is also important. ECE students need time to reflect upon their observations as they will be required to observe the child's significant learning and consider how they can respond. As observers, we have to learn how to effectively react to the things that we see children doing. This might feel difficult at first, but with regular practice ECE students will not only observe significant moments but be more able to predict how the child's play might unfold, thereby seeing the whole child.

Observations and Assessment

Assessment is the link between what we observe and what we plan for children. ECE students must ensure that it is both responsive and meets the child's needs. This involves thinking about our interpretations and interactions and how we respond to children. It is important that ECE students understand that young children need to have plenty of opportunities to engage in active play. Movement is critical to learning and will bring children into contact with the wider world. Babies, toddlers and young children will frequently explore toys and objects that encourage them to move. They may also talk about what they are doing. They also need time and space to rehearse and repeat newly acquired skills. Repetition should not be discouraged as children will often be observed using their existing knowledge in new ways. Children need opportunities to negotiate obstacles in their environment, to be talkative and be heard. With numbers all around them, they will repeat number words in songs and in play without yet having an understanding of them (Munn, 2009: 1). For example, if we observe Mathias (2 years, 9 months) at nursery counting cars by moving them one at a time from a table, walking across the room and giving them to his friend, would we concentrate on his number skills or step back and observe? Ultimately, children will need to draw on their first-hand experiences of numbers to support and challenge their thinking. An educator who was near to Mathias observed lots of mathematical language, like 'here's another one, that makes 1, 2, 3 altogether, here's one more...' but she did not ask him to join in counting or question him about how many. Instead, she allowed him to 'bank' all this language for future reference. Using her observations and knowledge of Mathias helped her to recognise that he was adding and taking away in his play, developing his understanding about quantity. The educator also noted that the importance of walking around was significant for Mathias. This seemed to help him establish one number for one thing and give him a sense that more things needed to have more walking involved, creating a fuller sense of what more means. One day, he will be able to use one finger to move each object as he counts it.

Noticing, Recognising and Responding

Each setting will use different techniques and approaches to inform teaching and learning. The New Zealand Early Years practice guide (2004), *Kei Tua o te Pae/Assessment for Learning* provides us with a very practical way to observe. In this guide it is not called observation but 'noticing, recognising and responding'. Each part of this three-step process is essential to the act of observing children. First, it involves ECE students picking up on a 'significant moment', then applying their professional knowledge and judgement to make sense of what they have seen before making decisions about how to respond. What is important to recognise is that noticing within our day-to-day practice is not a shallow action – rather, it is one that is embedded in the knowledge of what we see and hear, how we respond and what our relationships are with children. As Manning-Morton (2018: 11) explains: 'Noticing is not just about absorbing information at a superficial level, noticing in effective practice is about:

- perception – how we use our senses to notice
- attention – what we focus on, and
- attunement – how we tune in and empathise.'

Noticing is a vital part of the observation process. It is about how we perceive and interpret what we see and is the starting point for ECE students in noting a child's new learning. We can notice things like how a child deals with new experiences, whether they play in a group, what language they speak when with friends, or what they like to do in the role-play area. Noticing helps us to build up our understanding of individual children and awareness of what motivates or engages them – this can lead to new insights about them.

Recognising is also a vital and integral part of the observation process. It is of great importance to ECE students, who will need to explore and reflect on how they recognise and value children's learning. Observing is one part of the process – recognising, analysing, interpreting and acting upon what has been observed is another issue altogether. Recognising enables ECE students not only to tune into children but also to draw on and apply knowledge of how children think, feel and learn to their observations. Not recognising significant moments and progression can lead to inappropriate assessments and poor outcomes for children.

Responding is about how tuned in we are and our ability to immediately respond to children's emerging learning, needs and relationships in educationally worthwhile ways. ECE students will be expected to use observations to make accurate assessments about how to support children's learning further. Noticing where significant learning is taking place allows ECE students to make assessments about how to support or extend learning. This can be 'in the moment' or at a later point. How we respond is a key part of the observation process, particularly where actions to effectively support and extend learning are made immediately.

Doing Observations

For ECE students, collecting observations and acting upon them involves three important things (Louis, 2021). Primarily, there should be a well-prepared learning environment, both inside and outside, that supports the children within and just ahead of their developmental phase (Vygotsky, 1978). Providing a rich learning environment and resources will support the child as an active agent in their own learning in which they can express themselves (Froebel, 1887). The learning environment that ECE students create is central in ensuring that all children are involved and their input is valued. Observations of children's play and explorations are essential since they help students to 'recognise children's ideas and experiences' (McTavish, 2018: 14). Moreover, ECE students must use observations to build on children's known interests and support their learning, communication and learning styles.

Next, babies, toddlers and young children need to be offered meaningful learning experiences which are stimulating and engaging. If students observe that children are interested in a particular theme or things, they need to provide opportunities to support this. An example would be setting up the role-play area with cooking utensils if the student has observed that the children are playing pretend cooking games. Think about what cooking activities you might be able to get the children involved in. What other resources and materials could you add around the learning environment, both indoors and outdoors? This requires that students are interested in what children are doing and how they are learning, as they must think carefully about how they might encourage and support children's holistic development in socially and culturally appropriate ways. Students should make sure that the experiences provided reflect the cultures and lifestyle of the children and families that they work with and are not only 'Eurocentric', while also making sure that the experiences offered are relevant to all of the children in the setting.

ECE students working with young children also need to pay close attention to what they are doing in order to gain an understanding of their developing capabilities so that they can become attuned to them. This means thinking about what ideas the child might be exploring. Observation provides ECE students 'with a path to begin to get to know children well, to work alongside and with them, and to know when to give them space to reflect and act alone, or with other children using initiative' (Louis, 2021: 15). In other words, observation can provide a means of getting to know children well, in a way that influences your teaching and your developing relationship with them. This gives students insight into their interests, abilities, strengths, knowledge and skills, so that we are then more able to support, extend and embed their learning.

Reflection

ECE students will need to:

- Review their current approach and attitude towards systematically observing children. Is it focusing on the diverse ways children have of doing things and what they can do?
- Make sure that the observational approach taken captures the child's holistic development.
- Make observations of children's explorations meaningful and manageable so that they can be built on.
- Consider how best to use current observations of children at play as a tool to develop or support their thinking.
- Regularly participate in training to refresh existing knowledge and understanding of child development.

Conclusion

If ECE students are to observe babies, toddlers and young children in a meaningful way they will need to have an in-depth understanding of child development, including knowledge of how a typical child thinks, feels and learns. In this way, they will understand the needs of young children and the things they do at certain stages of their development. This means students basing observations upon what they know and appreciating how the child develops and learns, supported by understanding of what is already known about the child, their interests and focus, and what they can do. Whichever approach ECE students adopt, they need to use their observations to capitalise on children's interests, focus and strengths and support any weakness. Observations have value only when we put them to good use in building on children's interests, thereby guiding and facilitating learning and development.

References

Bartholomew, L. and Bruce, T. (1993) *Getting To Know You: Guide to Record-Keeping in Early Childhood Education and Care (0-8 Years Series)*. London: Hodder Education.

Flannery Quinn, S. and Manning, J. (2013) 'Recognising the ethical implications of the use of photography in Early Childhood educational settings'. *Contemporary Issues in Early Childhood,* 14(3): 270–8.

Froebel, F. (1887) *The Education of Man.* New York: Appleton.

Isaacs, S. (1930) *Intellectual Growth in Young Children.* London: Routledge and Sons.

Isaacs, S. (1929) *The Nursery Years.* London: Routledge and Sons.

Louis, S. (2021) 'Have observations become confused with recording?' *Early Education,* 94: 14–15.

Manning-Morton, J. (2018) 'Noticing, recognising, responding and reflecting: The process of observing infants and young children'. *Early Education,* 85: 11–13.

McTavish, A. (2018) 'The pirates! Using observation to support English as an Additional Language (EAL) through imaginative play'. *Early Education,* 84: 14–15.

Ministry of Education (2004) *Kei Tua o te Pae/Assessment for Learning: Early Childhood Exemplars.* New Zealand: Learning Media Limited. www.teaching-and-learning/ assessment-for-learning/kei-tua-o-te-pae accessed 10/09/21.

Munn, P. (2009) 'Parent Leaflet – The Maths Pyramid for Babies and Young Children', eduBuzz.org

Nutbrown, C. and Carter, C. (2010) 'The tools of assessment: Watching and learning' in G. Pugh and B. Duffy (eds), *Contemporary Issues in the Early Years* (5th edn). London: Sage.

Vygotsky, L.S. (1978) *Mind in Society: The Development of Higher Psychological Processes.* Cambridge, MA: Harvard University Press.

Whalley, M. (2017) *Involving Parents in their Children's Learning. A Knowledge-Sharing Approach* (3rd edn). London: Sage.

2
THE CYCLE OF OBSERVATION

Introduction

This chapter will touch on the practical element of observing and how educators can build it into their daily practice. It covers why, what, where and how to observe, the process of writing up observations and the purpose and uses of observation in record keeping. It will also explore unconscious bias. Different methods of observation and the pros and cons of these will be explored. Several formats will be introduced for readers to use in their own practice, such as narrative, Effective Early Learning Tracking (EEL) and sociograms. Connections will be made throughout this chapter with the Observe, Assess and Plan process of the UK's *Early Years Foundation Stage (EYFS), Curriculum for Excellence Foundation Phase Curriculum, Aistear* (Ireland) and *Kei Tua o te Pae/Assessment for Learning* (New Zealand).

Observations are part of a cycle of Observe, Assess and Plan. In practice, each of these elements are visible and are undertaken regularly. The observation cycle begins with describing children's learning. This means we need to pay attention to what we see and hear and describe the behaviours that make us sit up and take notice. It is also an opportunity to watch for what is new or different for a child.

Froebel (1782–1852) emphasises the importance of observing children. His observations show how children grow and develop through their self-activities, first-hand experiences and the people that they spend time with. For Froebel, observation is a necessary tool for teaching to be used to support children's learning sensitively. He states:

Observation of children is just as important for us too. In doing so we catch sight of our own far-off childhood which, like our own faces, we can only see in a mirror. Through our observations we come to understand ourselves and our own life, which then becomes for us an unbroken whole. (Froebel, in Lilley, 1967: 79)

The importance of this quotation is the way in which it makes us consider how our own reflective approach can, at times, superimpose our own recollections, understandings and aspirations onto the children we work with. This is not necessarily a bad thing. As Froebel suggests, it is a way of making sense of our own lives, as well as trying to get to grips with understanding children. However, students must be careful not to assume that the child being observed feels the same as them.

ECE students should be highly trained and understanding observations is part of this. When students get into the habit of regularly observing, it becomes second nature to follow and tune into the child's spontaneous and intrinsic motivations. Observations are a vital tool which provide information to help students respond to children's needs. ECE students can learn a lot about why and when children do certain things by having a thorough knowledge of child development and by watching what children do. Without this essential knowledge students can sometimes misinterpret what children are trying to tell them – this can make interactions with them difficult. Observation is a fundamental aspect of teaching and involves careful watching, listening, noticing, supporting and being connected to the child and the event.

Observation is What You See, Notice and Hear

> Jack (1 year) was observed holding a sun cream bottle to his ear while sitting in his buggy. Later, he propped a rectangular lid against a chair and seemed to be pretending to have a video call.

The next stage in the process is assessment – analysing or interpreting observations in order to increase insight into how children are learning. This means we need to consider what the observation tells us and what it means. In the example above, Jack is beginning to use one thing to stand in for something else. He has made a transition in moving from literal play to symbolic play.

The final stage is planning – what should be done with the information from the observation? It is important not to draw conclusions from a single observation. Good analysis is achieved from a range of observations across a number of different experiences and activities. Therefore, more observations of Jack in a variety of situations should be gathered and more open-ended resources added throughout the environment to support Jack's symbolic play.

Observe Children in a Range of Play Situations

- Inside and outdoors
- Playing alone

- Playing alongside
- Playing with other children in pairs or small groups
- Participating in larger groups
- Imaginative play
- Small world play
- Construction and block play
- Creative activities
- Physical activities

Observation practice should always lead to action being taken and such action can come in many different forms. Once ECE students have analysed their observations, they are in a good position to make a change to the immediate environment to support, embed and extend learning or to nourish an interest. Consider carefully how to respond and interact to support and extend learning and make assessments about how much and how well a child has learned. Babies, toddlers and young children behave very differently from adults. We should have realistic expectations of them and not expect them to act in the same way that we do. Children's learning and development is revealed in the way that they play with different resources and materials. Through reflecting on close observations in a variety of contexts we can better plan to help children to progress.

Moral Observations

Records of observations and assessments need to stand up to scrutiny and challenge by others. The relationships that we establish with children while we are observing them are important because they contribute towards developing a moral and ethical observation practice in which children come first. The writing up of an observation should not get in the way of how we respond to children or how supportive we are of them. ECE students have a pedagogical responsibility to be mindful of the child's voice and rights while they are carrying out observations.

It is important that ECE students take time to consider and reflect on whether they are acting in a moral way when they are observing young children. We need to question if our observations are really listening to children and looking at what their play has to tell us. Focusing observation on children's interests and the activities that they choose for themselves will help to ensure that we capture, value and respect what they do. This will further support understanding about why we observe and what we are recording. According to Brodie:

> Observing and interacting with young children is a pleasure and a privilege. Practitioners should be aware that being involved with children also means having responsibilities for their own actions and always being aware of the children's rights. This includes allowing the children not to be involved with activities: in brief, to act in a moral, ethical manner. (2013: 22)

This means that observing children only in adult-directed activities or getting a child to do a specific task just so that we can gather information is not moral. These kinds of observations can have an impact on their validity and reliability.

Why Observe?

We observe babies, toddlers and young children for several different reasons. These include getting a better picture of children's understanding, support for learning, assessment and planning, and developing our own practice. It is vital that ECE students approach their work from a position of enquiry rather than judgement. It is also necessary to continue to draw on knowledge of child development to undertake a range of observations. Nutbrown (1996: 45) makes a useful point: 'Children approach their learning with wide eyes and open minds, so their educators too need wide eyes and open minds to see clearly and to understand what they see.'

Ultimately, we observe children to gain knowledge of what they can do: to understand their strengths and be aware of their weaknesses; to understand where a child likes to learn best; to understand a child's preferred way of learning and their stage of development. Observing helps us to learn about a child and predict and recognise their behaviour. It will be necessary to pose some questions to help us get to know the children being observed. For example, what does the child like to do? What is the child's focus? What does the child find difficult? These questions will help us to learn something about the child's skills and interests.

What to Observe?

- Children's interests
- Talking, moving, facial expressions
- Levels of involvement – is the child just going through the motions?
- Children persisting with difficulty, challenging themselves
- Children communicating with others
- Children taking responsibility
- Stages of child development
- Areas of learning and development
- Evidence of the characteristics of effective learning, particularly around curiosity and making links, and developing their own ideas and strategies
- Schemas
- Emerging learning

Observations must be a factual account of what we see and hear. They can include what the child actually says, but not what we think they are saying. Louis and Betteridge say:

Our observations of children are like stories – sometimes our stories are factual, at other times they are based on what we think we see, our attitudes and our interpretation of children's behaviour. How likely are we to put our assumptions, beliefs and expectations into our story in positive and/or negative ways? (2020: 2)

Keeping the observation factual will help us to challenge our perceptions and show what is really happening, as opposed to what we assume might be happening. The following observations demonstrate this point.

Observation 1:

Ella watches and feels the water pouring from the jug through the funnel and her fingers. She seems interested in the flow. She watches intently as the water disappears through the funnel.

Observation 2:

Ella is fascinated by play with water and enjoys getting wet.

Observation 1 tells us much more about what Ella does and is interested in, while Observation 2 tells us about the observer's personal judgement – Ella enjoys getting wet.

Nutbrown (1996: 47) suggests that 'if educators are blinkered, having tunnel vision, they may not have the full picture – so it's not simply a case of understanding what is seen but it is first crucial to see what is really happening and not what adults suppose to be happening'. Observations must be factual and highlight learning – the significant things that a child is doing (Fawcett, 2009).

Close and thoughtful observation of young children enables ECE students to better understand their competencies as well as gaining insight into how and where children like to learn. Children learn best when they are busy doing things. It is through their play and exploration that they show us how they are developing as competent and able learners and we need to be able to describe this learning.

Prompts for Describing Learning

- What materials does the child play with?
- What do they do with the materials?
- What problems do they encounter and how do they solve them?
- What are the child's interests?
- What do they like to do?

- What choices do they make?
- With whom do they play?
- What kind of play do they choose?
- How do they communicate verbally and non-verbally?
- What do they say?
- What kind of questions do they ask?
- To what extent do they use language to describe events and tell stories?
- What kind of experiences do they share?
- Do they get involved in pretend play?
- What do they represent symbolically in models, drawings and paintings?

Being aware of these prompts will help to ensure that we gather meaningful observations that show children as active and capable learners.

Observing Learning

When we observe play and learning we might include observations where children are showing an interest; coping with a new experience by using existing knowledge in different ways; persevering with challenges or difficulties; establishing a relationship with children or adults; or showing self-discipline. Whatever learning we observe, we must describe what it is that the child does. Nutbrown (1996: 47) suggests: 'Adults need to make detailed and sensitive observations to really "see" what children are doing, to make sense of their actions, to recognise their achievement and to create further learning opportunities.' Our observations need to be child-centred, illustrate development and be responsive in ways which support and capture children's play and learning.

Assessment

Assessment is the link between what we observe and what we plan. It is a key aspect of daily activities in Early Childhood education and includes how we interpret learning. Assessment is not just talking about a child's phonic knowledge and number symbol recognition. Assessment is being able to talk about individual children at length and with great personal detail about their temperament, interests, skills, abilities, preferred way of learning, culture at home and their interactions with others, while citing whole observations where their play illustrates learning. Assessment is knowing children's passions and desires, their language patterns, what makes them laugh and what they avoid doing. Assessment is about really knowing and understanding children and how they think and learn. Ultimately, assessment is a window into the child's world, where we are both learners. Children's learning is the most exciting thing – the way that they pass through stages in such different ways is fascinating.

When we think about assessment, we should not always regard it as something to be used as a tool but as a privileged opportunity to really look at and listen to a child, to find out how they are thinking and making sense of the world so that we can come away with more understanding. It is a bit like reading a novel where the author is able to illuminate why a character does what they do.

Formative Assessment

This is related to the ongoing assessment of children's progression that enables us to understand what they know and can do. In other words, formative assessment looks at how much a child is learning throughout the *Early Years Foundation Stage, Curriculum for Excellence, Foundation Phase Curriculum*, or *Aistear: the Early Childhood Curriculum Framework* (2009). Also known as assessment for learning, it is carried out frequently to gather information about the child to determine what is needed to support them. Assessments can take place through different sources of evidence, such as observation, questioning, conversations and interactions. This kind of assessment encourages ECE students to reflect.

Summative Assessment

This is an assessment of the child's process of learning that determines whether or not they have reached a learning goal. Summative assessment determines how much a child has learned throughout the *Early Years Foundation Stage*; for example, has the child mastered a particular mathematical concept at the end of term? In England, children are measured against a number of learning goals and this is completed at the end of the Foundation Stage.

Interpreting Learning

Our interpretations of children's learning are not neutral or value free – they are subject to our own preconceptions and understanding of what we observe. We can increase our objectivity if we focus our observations on describing what we see and hear, and this should provide us with enough useful information. Dubiel (2008: 93) highlights that the act of interpreting is driven by a set of influences. He suggests that interpretation 'is based on our own agendas and preoccupations, mediating children's activity through our own values and principles, defining what is considered important and driving the provision, interactions and support that follows'.

Observations can and should lead us to question and think more deeply about what we see and hear. As we interpret our observations, we make important decisions about how much and how well a child has learned. These interpretations influence our interactions and the learning environment we create to support and extend learning. If we interpret children's actions based only on our own agenda, we may unwittingly limit what we offer them. Our interpretations are not only connected to our descriptions of a child's play but also to our personal values about the play we are observing. ECE students will need to reflect regularly on their observations of the child. One way to do this is to participate in robust group discussions with colleagues, unpicking the observed play and sharing interpretations from different perspectives about the child's thoughtful actions (Louis, 2020).

It is vital that that ECE students make time to think about and interpret their observations so that they can reflect on the way in which a child is learning. This is a central part of the Observe, Assess and Plan cycle. For example, Raphael (10 months) frequently plays a game where he sits at the top of two steps with a basket of balls of different sizes, weights and textures and throws them down. When the balls behave differently, Raphael can be seen wondering why they have not all gone to the bottom step as he expected them to. It is clear from this observation that Raphael's thoughtful actions of throwing the balls is supporting his learning and thinking.

ECE students must get into the habit of thinking about what they are observing as children play and explore and ask themselves questions to help interpret their behaviour, such as, what is the child thinking? How thoughtful are their actions? What is the goal, aim or purpose? What questions are they trying to work out? How can we support them? These questions are key to the observation process.

Unconscious Bias

Unconscious bias is when we make snap judgements about the things that we see children doing. Often, our unconscious bias may not chime with our consciously held beliefs and this is why we need to be aware of it. Being mindful of our unconscious bias matters, whether it is in relation to race, gender, sexuality, disability or class.

ECE students need to reflect on their own unconscious bias and think about the challenges it poses in observation, assessment and planning. The subjectivity of the observer and how they analyse observations might embrace a range of perspectives. Our observations are subject to unconscious bias because they are based on our preconceptions and interpretation of what we can see. We need to be aware that unconscious bias can lead to incorrect assessments, resulting in us not following children's interests or planning for them appropriately, thereby affecting their development and learning. For example, a non-biased assessment would record Lucy saying she was making 'a castle with a glass roof' after spending 25 minutes in the block area using the same size of rectangular blocks to build with. A biased assessment would record that Lucy enjoys the activities that boys like.

Our unconscious biases are often deeply ingrained in the feelings, attitudes and beliefs that help us to navigate the world, but they can lead us to prejudice and unfair treatment of others. There are several types of unconscious bias – knowing what they are will help us to see the complex subtlety at play.

Affinity bias is when we are more comfortable with people who look like us, dress like us, act like us and behave like us, because they are familiar. We may share many similarities with them. Unconsciously, we may treat children and families who do not look like us very differently. For example, do we react differently to some children's non-compliant behaviour than others? Or are we more likely to make allowances for children and families who we have an affinity with?

Confirmation bias is when we only consider information that backs up our preconceptions about children and their families. This affects our ability to recall and remember information about positive encounters with them. For example, if we believe that a child is not engaging in learning, we may only look for evidence that confirms this. If we observe the child at circle time and see that they are not singing with the rest of the group, we will use that information to confirm our thoughts about the child, even if we had also observed the child making compost outside and singing the same song as they played.

Attribution bias is when we focus on the child's characteristics rather than giving them the benefit of the doubt. For instance, if a child that we believe is clumsy knocks over another child, we may automatically say that the child is clumsy, or did it deliberately, without knowing the full story. We will blame aspects of the child's attributes rather than accepting that it was an accident because the child tripped over their shoelaces. We must be careful with attribution bias not to label children with words like 'clumsy' or 'troublemaker' because these words tell us little about the child's activity or behaviour. Labels can be dangerous – they often stick and young children can begin to think of themselves in that way.

Non-Biased Observations

We can counter our biases by making sure that our observation and assessment skills are as good as they can be. We need to have systems in place to check that we are not making stereotypical and biased judgements and decisions.

Ensure that planning starts with observation and that you have time to reflect on what has been observed. All of our assessments about young children's learning need to be reliable – we therefore need to consider if we know the children well enough to make correct and dependable judgements about their development, learning and progression. It is important that ECE students reflect on the different types of unconscious bias. Be open, honest and unafraid of how uncomfortable the subject matter is. It is important to explore the subject, knowing that it is normal to have unconscious bias. We need to be OK with challenging it in ourselves when we recognise it and seek to develop our awareness of it. Our biases determine who gets to excel, who is permitted to stand out, who is referred to as a disrupter and who is put aside for being disruptive.

Recording Observations

Recording observations requires ECE students to write about the child's starting point and past learning. When writing an observation, ECE students need to reflect on the language used – try to avoid words such as enjoyed, likes, hates and loves. Fawcett reminds us to be aware of our personal assumptions and judgements, saying:

> Learning how to observe and find the words, the 'right' kind of language, to describe complex dynamic behaviour is more difficult than one might think. It is an art, almost akin to writing a short story, though this is not fiction, even if everyone is writing from within their own perspective. (2009: 53)

Our observations will change from child to child.

According to Louis:

> Gathering observations and acting on them involves three things. Firstly, a well organised learning environment, both indoors and outdoors, that supports the children within and just ahead of their developmental phase (Vygotsky, 1978). Secondly, that children are offered meaningful learning experiences which are socially and culturally appropriate, stimulating and engaging. Thirdly, the adults working with them need to be able to pay close attention to what they are doing in order to gain an understanding of children's developing capabilities and to become attuned to them. (2021: 15)

Ways of Recording Observations – Learning Stories

Carr and Lee (2012) suggest that learning stories are effective ways of documenting learning, using mutual relationships between the child, people and the environment. These record children's learning using narrative, video and photographs. Stories focus on what a child can do and build on the child's sense of identity and belonging to a community.

Time sampling – An observation is taken at set intervals whatever the child is doing, for example, in the sandpit outdoors, pushing a cart outside, at the clay table indoors. These give a useful picture of the child's day.

Event sampling – This is another form of observation of behaviour that focuses on what happens before and after the behaviour being investigated and helps to identify if there are triggers or rewards.

Frequency sampling – A record is made of how often a behaviour occurs, such as playing with other children, biting, or feeling threatened rather than talking about what they are feeling. These observations are particularly helpful in identifying what is needed in order to help children. Educators can then help children to enjoy concentrated attention in solitary play with small world materials as well as play with their peers or offer useful words to deal with emotionally difficult situations such as sharing or needing a turn.

Effective Early Learning Tracking (EEL) – Pascal and Bertram (1997) suggest that EEL tracking increases and maintains the quality of children's learning. It helps to support an educator's levels of involvement in children's learning as well as tracking the child's and educator's engagement and involvement in the learning process. This is a useful and rigorous way of evaluating and improving provision but requires specific training.

Check list – This is a limited and often narrow list of what is to be observed and, if present, ticked or coded. The observer ignores what is not on the list. Check lists yield little information but demand intense effort to complete them.

Anecdotal – This is a useful method because what is observed is not written down on the spot but recalled at the end of the session. A photograph or video might be taken and written notes added later in the day to enhance the observation. This quiet gathering of thoughts about what children are doing and how they communicate is not intrusive for the baby or child, who are often not at ease when they see adults with notepads observing what they are doing. Part of the skill of the observer is to be able to stand back discreetly and watch and listen, so that the situation is as normal as possible for the child being observed.

Narrative – These observations are written on the spot and taken at regular intervals. They can be ongoing, so they are more reliable in accuracy than anecdotal records (Isaacs, 1930). How the baby or child is communicating or talking and what they are engaged in at the time is recorded. As they are made over a longer period, they can often reveal repeated actions and behaviours in different contexts. The observation will be written, but photographs and video may also be taken. Narrative observations are more time consuming but using Post-it notes is helpful – these can be expanded later in the day and sent digitally to parents and colleagues. Children might become self-conscious and uncomfortable if they feel closely scrutinised, which needs to be sensitively acknowledged and respected. Audio recordings are really useful as they also inform our observations (Paley, 1992). They capture speech and conversations where the adult can be involved and still retain an accurate record.

Sociogram – Students can use different methods of observation to elicit the knowledge they want from play and social situations. Sociograms are one example and can include both child and adult social interaction. A sociogram is a method of observation for monitoring the interactions and relationships within a group. Sociograms are useful when we need a more focused observation that will enable us to track the child's interactions. We can use them to observe when the child arrives, who they interact with, where interaction occurs and what happens, and at what time of the day. Sociograms can provide us with a deeper understanding about the child's relationships with others.

Reflection

Students will need to:

- Start small and take tiny steps into this ongoing process.
- Make sure that they have a notebook or Post-it notes to record what children are actually saying and doing.
- Regularly participate in sharing observations with colleagues (planning meetings are a good place to do this). Find out what colleagues think about the observation. Can they see any connections with play patterns in different contexts?
- Always reflect on the questions that observations raise for colleagues and use planning meetings to find out more. Does the perspective of colleagues match yours or is it different?
- Reflect on the expectations and outcomes of their observations and assessments to ensure that they have equal aspirations for all children and not just the ones that they have an affinity with.

Conclusion

We need to link our records to children's progress, as well as review what we offer them, whatever method of observation we adopt in practice. Our records need to be useful if we are to be helpful to children and their families. This can be a difficult and challenging aspect of our role, but we must find manageable ways to do this. It is useful to have regular reviews with parents, making the sharing of observations with them part of the process of Observe, Assess and Plan, or finding ways for parents to be able to share their observations at the same time in a mutual exchange of information. Ultimately, we need to link our analysed observations of individual children to our planning and provision. In this way, we can ensure that what we provide for children is relevant and supports their unique path of development and learning.

References

Brodie, K. (2013) *Observation, Assessment and Planning in the Early Years – Bringing It All Together*. London: McGraw-Hill Education.

Carr, M. and Lee, W. (2012) *Learning Stories: Constructing Learner Identities in Early Education*. London: Sage.

Dubiel, J. (2008) 'Tiaras may be optional – The truth isn't: The Early Years Foundation Stage and accurate assessment' in S. Featherstone (ed.), *Like Bees, Not Butterflies: Child-Initiated Learning in the Early Years*. London: A&C Black.

Fawcett, M. (2009) *Learning Through Child Observation*. London: Jessica Kingsley.

Isaacs, S. (1930) *Intellectual Growth in Young Children*. London: Routledge and Sons.

Lilley, I. (1967) *Friedrich Froebel: A Selection from his Writings*. Cambridge: Cambridge University Press.

Louis, S. (2020) *How to Use Work Group Supervision to Improve Early Years Practice*. London: Routledge.

Louis, S. (2021) 'Have observations become confused with recording?' *Early Education*, 94: 14–15.

Louis, S. and Betteridge, H. (2020) *Unconscious Bias in the Observation, Assessment and Planning Process*. Foundation Stage Forum.

National Council for Curriculum and Assessment (NCCA) (2009) *Aistear: The Early Childhood Curriculum Framework*. Dublin: National Council for Curriculum and Assessment.

Nutbrown, C. (1996) *Respectful Educators, Capable Learners: Young Children's Rights and Early Education*. London: Taylor and Francis.

Paley, V.G. (1992) *You Can't Say You Can't Play*. Cambridge, MA: Harvard University Press.

Pascal, C. and Bertram, A.D. (1997) *The Effective Early Learning Project: Case Studies in Improvement*. London: Hodder & Stoughton.

Vygotsky, L.S. (1978) *Mind in Society: The Development of Higher Psychological Processes*. Cambridge, MA: Harvard University Press.

3

THE NETWORK FOR LEARNING

Introduction

The term 'network for learning' was first coined in 1996 by Tina Bruce, who defines it as 'a network of development and learning which is coordinated by play' (Bruce, 1996: 7). The network for learning is chiefly concerned with all the ways that children learn and includes exploration, discovery, experimentation, repetition, observation and listening. It has many aspects that interact, overlap and influence each other in a complex network that supports children in their learning trajectory. It represents a combination of the many diverse ways that children learn through their own efforts and integrates all that they know and can do. Bruce suggests that being able to recognise aspects of this network can help students to identify what is happening for a child. Aspects of the network may appear as a game, telling us that a child might be using rules. It may be expressed as a representation of something that a child might have seen, telling us that they are recalling a past experience.

ECE students will be required to observe what is happening for a child. They also need to understand how children are learning. Recognising the network for learning will help students to see and understand the complexities and connections in children's play. Ultimately, the network provides students with insight into the child.

First-Hand Experiences

Children learn through their first-hand experiences as they interact with people, objects and the environment. In responding to these experiences, children will use whatever resources are available to them, such as curiosity about what will happen to sand if it is put into water, or they may recreate real experiences (Zosh et al., 2017). For example, Anna-Louise (3 years, 9 months) was observed using her first-hand experience of going to a café with her grandparents in her pretend play, in which she made tea for her friends from soil and water. It is in this way, through actively exploring a range of objects and materials that they come across, that children may test out their environment and alter or modify their thinking to meet their own needs. Unless babies, toddlers and young children have first-hand experience, they cannot connect their learning to life and what they know about it. First-hand experiences are concrete experiences and they help children not just to learn but also to solve problems, such as finding out what happens when they climb up onto something and how to get down.

Babies and toddlers will frequently be observed cooking, putting baby to bed, going shopping, parking the car and talking on the telephone. They use everyday real experiences to help them to relate and connect to the world. As their experiences continue to grow at home and in the setting, their play and explorations begin to expand the details by enacting the parts that are significant to them in a literal or symbolic way – one example might be putting the doll to bed because it has been naughty. Bruce (1996) reminds us that children have not occupied the planet or lived for as long as us – they can only learn through the experiences they have gained from the people that they interact with and everything that is around them.

Struggle

At times, our observations of babies, toddlers and young children capture their struggles. As we watch, we may want to rush in and offer our help before they have developed the skills to work things out for themselves. However, we must be careful not to intervene too quickly and make the experience too easy to achieve, thereby preventing them from reaching their possibilities. That said, ECE students need to know just when and how to give support or stand back and observe. Struggle can help children to develop problem-solving skills and increase their confidence and capacity to reach their goals, such as a baby crawling towards an object using their whole body to reach or get closer to it.

Struggle and challenge are good for children's growth and development. Struggle teaches children important lessons of self-discipline – to keep trying and not give up. The process of their struggle enables them to take on challenges that they work out for themselves through trial and error. Struggle can also offer children different learning opportunities in managing a range of different feelings and emotions, such as frustration. Struggle is important to learning as it helps children to persevere with difficulty in order to develop their strengths. For example, over several days Oscar (10 months) was observed in the baby walker struggling to get it to move. Although his first strategy did not work, he still persisted. Through the process of his struggle, he worked out that he could use his weight to make the walker move. Similarly, 12-month-old Georgia struggled to work out the order of stacking cups. But she did not give up – she chose to persist with stacking cups over several days until she was satisfied.

Exploration and Discovery

Babies, toddlers and young children learn best by building on what they are interested in and what they know they can already do. Exploration leads to discoveries being made about the way different materials and objects behave. In one instance, Ruby (10 months) played a game from her highchair where she held and then let go of a selection of balls of different sizes, textures and weights. Through her exploration of dropping them she discovered that some balls behave differently from others. Ruby's first-hand experiences will act as an anchor to finding out more about cause and effect. If children are encouraged to explore a range of resources and materials, they will begin to make discoveries for themselves. While playing with the play dough, Shari (4 years) found that the round birthday cake she had made could be cut into four pieces, then eight. Exploration enables children to use resources and materials in a way that allows them to see what they can do with them. In this way, children begin to make connections with ideas from their experiences. However, we cannot know for certain what a child understands from their explorations, or what discoveries they have made, unless we take time to observe, listen to and question them.

Experimentation and Repetition

Experimentation and repetition are important for young children. Experimentation helps children to make links between their ideas and actions. It also helps them to begin to understand how they can make things happen. Schedules and routines help children to experience the same thing happening to them over and over again. This enables them to make predictions about what will happen next. ECE students need to capture children's experimentation in their observations and describe how children manipulate materials to create things for themselves. For example, James (2 years, 4 months) was frequently observed handling play dough. He would experiment by breaking it into small pieces then manipulate the pieces in his hand before making a ball. This observation can be analysed for what it tells us about the child's interests and enables us to plan further opportunities to support their experimentation. We may observe children experimenting physically by moving their bodies or playthings around in different ways. Children will not only experiment with materials but also with language, using words new, old and invented as well as songs and rhymes. Sand and water play offers children wonderful opportunities to explore through their senses as they experiment with filling and emptying buckets of sand or pouring water through funnels. If children are to become familiar with these experiences they will need to be repeated until they are able to predict what will happen. When we observe children closely we will notice that much of their play is repetitive and of the child's own choosing.

> Day after day Mia (2 years, 1 month) would spend long periods of time drizzling glue into a small pot from two different heights. First, she would raise the glue brush to eye level and watch the glue drip. Then she would raise her hand just above her head and watch the glue fall again, all the time noticing the changes in consistency as it drizzled from different heights. Mia's observations of the glue are important as they will support her continuing understanding and her thinking.

Repetition allows children to recall what they know and can do, supporting them to test out and develop their ideas. Kryczka (2020) reinforces the notion that repetition is the basis of much learning. She cites literacy specialist Judith Wright, saying: 'A baby needs 1,000 repetitions to learn a word; by the time he's a toddler, he might need 50 repetitions; and when he's in kindergarten, he may need only a few repetitions to master it because the brain connections have been laid out.' Observations by ECE students of children experimenting and repeating will help them to develop their understanding about the child's thinking and problem-solving skills.

Practising Newly Acquired Skills

Students may observe children intentionally practising a skill in order to improve their performance. It does not matter what skill children choose to practise – the development of any skill is affected by how much they are able to apply it in their everyday experiences. However, practising newly acquired skills is not the same as simply repeating a set of actions. Repetition alone cannot improve a child's performance. Practising and applying skills includes repetition, rehearsal and attention, which leads to skills being enhanced. Although other factors such as ability, motivation and opportunity can affect a child's performance, practice is necessary. Children will need plenty of meaningful opportunities to practise their skills over and over again as this plays an important role in children's overall development. When a child has mastered something, such as being able to pour their own water or dress themselves, they know how to do it and will need further meaningful opportunities to develop proficiency and confidence. Each time children practise a skill it is an opportunity for them to apply their expertise in known and new situations. It also helps children to make connections in their learning. We need to give children plenty of feedback and encouragement in their efforts to practise new skills by telling them clearly what they have done well.

Competence

Babies, toddlers and young children need everyday experiences to develop their competence. They like to take part in and contribute to the things that they see adults around them doing, all the time working hard to develop their competence.

> Olly (4 years) asked if he could help to cut some wood. He was observed in the garden using an adult-size hacksaw, positioning his foot on the wood so that it would not move. Later, he was seen using a much smaller saw to show his two-year-old brother Samuel how to use the tools, helping him to develop his technique. He said that he was using the smaller saw with Samuel because it would be easier for him to do it. Even though Samuel did not ask for help, Olly knew how to make the experience easier for him.

Having these types of experiences will give children the confidence they need to explore further and take risks. ECE students will need to use their observation skills and knowledge to know when to step in and support them and when to step back and watch. However, if adults take control of risky activities, such as using real tools, they may unwittingly send out messages to children that will undermine their confidence and lead them to assume that we do not think that they are able to do it themselves. It is important that ECE students reflect on the opportunities that they offer children to develop their competence.

Mastery

Children need to learn how to move their bodies easily and confidently. This means developing both their small and large muscles so that they co-ordinate and work together. At first, a baby may pick up an object with their whole hands. Once they have developed and mastered this skill, the baby will be able to pick things up with their fingers. Mastery is reached through children having ample opportunity to practise and repeat, as well as time to wallow in what they are doing. This will also enable children to set goals for themselves. If we notice children tackling challenging things, we need to encourage their efforts to persist. This kind of encouragement will also help children to feel more able to master a wide range of new skills, such as social situations and language skills, and using cutlery and writing tools. We need to be able to recognise and reflect on how children's skills develop and change as they grow and be available to promote them. The process of analysing and interpreting our observations will inform us as to what skills children have mastered and what they still need help with. This means continual assessment, collecting systematic and varied observations of how they have developed over time in a variety of activities and contexts. Furthermore, our assessment of children's changing skills should include ongoing dialogue with parents. The next example illustrates how children can master a skill through their self-chosen play.

> Nine-month-old Amy was repeatedly observed exploring a metal bowl with great interest. She soon became aware that the movements she made with her hands could turn the bowl over. Amy smiled and laughed every time she turned the bowl over successfully.

Control

The play that babies, toddlers and young children select for themselves is important because it allows them to be in control. Allowing them to follow their intrinsic motivation and interests gives them permission to learn in their own unique way. Through their self-chosen play, children learn about the world and themselves. When children are in control of their play they will create challenges, test their theories and make mistakes, as well as finding new ways of doing things. When children choose what they play with, they will use their play to express their feelings in a variety of different ways.

Jody's parents recently got married, so Jody (4 years, 3 months) chose to play a wedding game. She was in control of the rules of the game. She pretended she was going to the airport to pick up her husband. She made rules with pretend children about what would happen when she got back from the airport. The more Jody played this game, the more elaborate it got – she eventually had two children, Flower and Timmy, and a dog named Barney. Bruce (1987) makes the point that play is a vehicle which children use in order to develop and learn and we must be mindful not to take over. For play to be meaningful for children it has to be in their control – it should be free from adults deciding what they should play and how they should play.

Wallowing in Feelings, Ideas and Relationships

Children will need plenty of opportunities to explore and make sense of their feelings, ideas and relationships. It is important that ECE students are able to differentiate between them and recognise when they are being expressed in play, either individually or together. A child might express their feeling of 'fear' in their play – such as being afraid of the dark after having a nightmare – telling us that they are beginning to make sense of their anxieties. Children may express ideas while playing at shops, showing us how they are recalling and re-enacting their experiences, or they may play games in which they explore their relationships with parents or other children, using their past experiences to bring their own ideas alive in play. When we observe children, we need to be able to recognise what is happening as they will use their experiences in this way to help them to make up and enact stories to understand those experiences.

We need to notice and interpret what it is we are seeing when we observe children play out their feelings, ideas and relationships. Through exploring their own ideas in their play, children develop a better understanding of the thoughts and feelings that they are trying to figure out. Erica (3 years, 5 months) played out her ideas about being a cat pregnant with kittens. Erica pretended to be a cat and was heard discussing how many kittens she was going to have. She told Lewis, 'Pretend that we are kittens and you die. Pretend we have to bury you.' The learning activities and experiences that we offer to children need to reflect and link to their interests and ideas. We must observe the fine detail of their play closely to help them to make connections and sense of the world around them. For example, Faith (3 years) played alone with her teddy at nursery. She pretended to make the teddy go to the toilet and flush. She was overheard telling the teddy not to worry, it will be okay, but you do have to do it. Another example is Frankie (5 years, 9 months) playing a game with Sky called sleepover. Frankie is staying with her dad and he (Sky) lets her stay up late. Frankie is exploring her relationship between her father and herself and what it includes. Ultimately, play allows children to express themselves, helping them to manage their fears as well as work out how they feel about things. It is interesting to note that Erica actually had a kitten that died. Similarly, shortly before Faith's play was observed, she had been scared to use the nursery toilet. In this way, her play can be seen to be helping her to make sense of her feelings about going to the toilet, as it allowed her to re-enact the situation while her play enabled her to be completely in control. Frankie's parents had recently separated. It is possible to see how playing in this way enables children to recall their past experiences and make sense of them.

Metacognition

Metacognition is when a child is aware of and in control of their own cognitive processes. This is an important aspect of development and learning and includes a child's ability to focus their attention and use a range of strategies. In order to regulate themselves, children need to draw on a wide range of metacognitive approaches to help them to persist with challenges, review what they know, and interpret and recognise errors as opportunities for learning (Bronson, 2000).

Storying

Stories support the development of a child's disembedded thinking. When children are exposed to stories, they will create stories for themselves to represent their understanding of their experiences and use these stories to reflect on and act upon their knowledge. Through stories, students can extend children's thinking, helping them to adopt new knowledge and understanding and confirm their emotions. According to Nutbrown (2009: 115), this can help children connect with their own experiences that are located within the story. She suggests that, in this way, a 'match of meaning' occurs. She says: 'Such a match between that which children find important and the stories they read and hear makes a crucial difference between simply hearing a story and really listening with absorbed intent and making it part of their thinking.'

Games

Children learn much from playing games that have rules. Games can help children to learn how rules are made, how to keep them, how to negotiate and change them, and how to understand someone else's rules. Games also help children to understand and develop social skills. Such play can be physical or social – such as board games – or performance-type sport, mathematical or computer games.

Lamar (4 years, 3 months) was losing while playing a game of snakes and ladders with his brother Jordan (6 years). He suggested that, rather than climb up the ladder, maybe Jordan should go down the snake instead.

Representation

Children's representations are their way of not only expressing their experiences, but also a means of using different materials to correspond with what they know. According to Bruce (1996), representations are the child's way of holding on to their experiences, through making and creating products that can be kept, or stories, songs and dances that can be performed and enacted again and again. Representation is about the many different ways that children will show their thoughts and feelings in the things that they do and make. Some children will create stories, songs, dances and rhymes repeatedly to represent their understanding of their experience. These oral and dynamic representations are significant and important because they help children to understand what happens next in the sequence of a dance, song, story or rhyme. Other children represent things graphically through drawing and painting. In this way, children make their ideas more visual to us. Representations can also be seen in children's models and constructions. Some children may be observed building and modifying things repeatedly or using materials such as clay or dough to represent their ideas. Ultimately, children use their representations to show us what they know. McKellar (1957: 117) suggests that 'imagination is the rearrangement of past experiences in new and fascinating ways'.

Imitation

Imitation is when a child copies the behaviours, sounds and actions of people around them. Imitation is a vital part of how babies, toddlers and young children learn and develop skills. It involves closely watching what people do, interpreting it, and being able to recall it. Imitation requires a child to use perceptual, cognitive and social knowledge. This is an important aspect of the network for learning – through imitating, children can show us what knowledge and understanding they have. Gopnik et al. (1990) suggest that imitation starts early with newborns. They say:

> At first glance this ability to imitate might seem curious and cute but not deeply significant. But if you think about it for a minute, it is actually amazing that there are no mirrors in the womb, newborns have never seen their own face, so how do they know whether their tongue is inside or outside their mouths? (1999: 30)

This is in the context of the newborn imitating the father in 'the social baby'. This suggests that imitation does not just occur by accident but is deliberate and used by the child for their own purpose. Nate (9 months) observed another child playing with a new toy. A few days later, Nate was seen to explore the toy and imitate the same actions he had seen the other child doing. This involves children thinking about what they imitate so that they can interact and connect to others in specific ways. Ryan (3 years, 9 months) imitated his grandfather shaving in front of the mirror. Ryan used a vibrating toy to represent the shaver, deliberately imitating the actions of his grandfather in order to learn how to shave himself. According to Gopnik et al., the art of imitating the actions of another enables children to search for knowledge and act it out. Imitation is also a mode of communication. If you imitate someone, you are saying: 'I have seen/heard you and it was like this'.

Symbolic Play

Symbolic play is when a child will make one thing stand in for another, such as a tin becoming a cup. Symbolic play often begins with what I describe as Pretend Play 1, or literal play (Louis, 2020). This is when children take experiences from their daily life, such as being put to bed, and then re-enact them. During this stage of development children initially tend to use literal, real and concrete objects to represent putting the baby to bed, such as a teddy or a doll, because they do not yet understand the meaning of symbols and abstract thinking. Pretend Play 2 is when children use an abstract object or materials to represent the real thing. If they are pretending to cook, they may use mud or some other material to symbolically represent the food, as opposed to having real food, such as in Pretend Play 1. In Pretend Play 2, children are using symbolic items to think, feel and remember in imaginative and abstract ways (Bruce et al., 2017). They no longer have to have the real object present for them to play. Sometimes we might observe children transitioning between Pretend Play 1 and 2.

Fantasy F play relates to how children act out real roles such as being mummy, daddy, teacher, shopkeeper or doctor. Children may rehearse any of these future roles in their pretend play, but this does not necessarily mean that they are going to take up such roles later on in life. Sometimes we may observe children playing cops and robbers – this kind of play theme helps children to deal with moral issues of good versus bad in meaningful ways. We should be careful not to stop this kind of play, even if we are uncomfortable dealing with its themes. Phantasy Ph play is about when children pretend to be, for example, a fairy, cat, dog or dinosaur. It is called Phantasy Ph because children are pretending to be things that they cannot be in real life.

Play

According to Bruce (1996), play has many aspects, co-ordinating and bringing together different learning in the network and helping children to realise what they know and understand to make connections. Piaget (1962) suggests that a child's intelligence develops from the extent to which they are stimulated through their play and exploration. He believes that play helps children to develop their logical thinking.

> Abbas (3 years, 1 month) was observed at the water tray, pouring jugs of water while singing one, two, three, four, five. At first, his counting did not correspond with the amounts that he was pouring. After many encounters of playing with the water, Abbas came to understand how to match numbers to quantity.

In their play, children build on their previous experiences and make predictions based on what they already know, leading to understanding. It is in this way that children build up their logical thinking.

Why are Observations in the Network for Learning So Important?

The network for learning helps ECE students to recognise how children are learning through their own efforts and self-initiated play activities. When students observe children deeply engaged or playing symbolically then this is normally an indicator that the network for learning is present. If students are observing children and they are unsure if they can see any of the network for learning, then it is best to keep observing and thinking. If students are clear that they have seen enough of the network for learning present in children's play, then they can make decisions as to how much autonomy and support to give a child (Bruce, Louis and McCall, 2014). As students observe children actively doing things for themselves, they should reflect on how the child's efforts lead them to reasoning and understanding (Froebel, 1887). Bruce (1996) urges ECE students to observe, support and extend children's play and explorations. The network for learning provides students with useful details about the kind of learning that is going on for the child.

Reflection

Students need to:

- Reflect on how their observations are making children's learning visible. Do your observations value the child's way of approaching the world? Have you noticed any play strategies for learning or symbolic and imaginative play?
- Recognise that children's first-hand experiences are the richest source from which we can teach them. How are you using your observations to learn and make connections about how the child is learning and thinking? Are you creating enough opportunities for children to make connections in their learning?
- Reflect on how they are helping children to learn. How are you helping them to develop competence, mastery and control?
- Look at video clips of children from birth to eight years. Siren Films have some great ones without narrative so that you can practise doing observations.

Conclusion

The network for learning has many aspects and, through play, provides learning for children in a number of different but interrelated ways. Each aspect of the network enables different connections to be made, leading to children becoming competent and able learners. ECE students must therefore look more closely at the things that children choose to do and learn from them. What children gain through the network for learning has no boundaries because it is inevitably co-ordinated by play, which is one of the most important aspects of human development (Froebel, 1887). In the next chapter, we explore the 12 features of play which help us to articulate how a child is learning.

References

Bronson, M.B. (2000) *Self-Regulation in Early Childhood: Nature and Nurture*. New York: Guilford Press.

Bruce, T. (1987) *Early Childhood Education*. London: Hodder & Stoughton.

Bruce, T. (1996) *Helping Young Children to Play*. London: Hodder & Stoughton.

Bruce, T., Hakkarainen, P. and Bredikyte, M. (2017) (eds) *The Routledge International Handbook of Early Childhood Play*. London: Routledge. pp. 87–96.

Bruce, T., Louis, S. and McCall, G. (2014) *Observing Young Children*. London: Sage.

Froebel, F. (1887) *The Education of Man*. New York: Appleton.

Gopnik, A., Meltzoff, A.N. and Kuhl, P.K. (1999) *The Scientist in the Crib: Mind, Brains, and How Children Learn*. New York, NY: William Morrow & Company.

Kryczka, C. (2020) 'Again, Again! Why Your Kids Want to do the Same Activity Over and Over'. *Today's Parent Online*.

Louis, S. (2020) *How to Use Work Group Supervision to Improve Early Years Practice*. London: Routledge.

McKellar, P. (1957) *Imagination and Thinking: A Psychological Analysis*. London: Cohen and West.

Nutbrown, C. (2009) *Threads of Thinking: Schemas and Young Children's Learning*. London: Sage.

Piaget, J. (1962) *Play, Dreams and Imitation in Childhood*. New York: Norton.

Zosh, J.M., Hopkins, E.J., Jensen, H., Liu, C., Neale, D., Hirsh-Pasek, K., Solis, S.L. and Whitebread, D. (2017) 'Learning Through Play: A Review of the Evidence'. *LEGO Foundation*.

4
THE 12 FEATURES OF PLAY

Introduction

Professor Tina Bruce (1991, 2015) identifies 12 features to help us recognise the most obvious characteristics of young children's learning through play. The 12 features of play give ECE students further insight into how children are learning and they can be used with the network for learning as a tool to evaluate the quality of experiences that we offer them.

The first feature states: 'In their play, children use first-hand experiences they have had in life.'

As we previously talked about, experience is important for learning. Piaget and Inhelder (1969) suggest that first-hand experiences are vital for children to learn, to think and to construct knowledge. When children have the opportunity to handle natural everyday objects in their learning environment, such as stones or pebbles, they advance in their knowledge of the physical properties. The more children experiment and repeat their explorations, they will learn that some stones are heavy, others are light, some are smooth, others are rough, rounded or sharp. In other words, young children will learn these concepts, not through being taught, but through their first-hand experience (Zosh et al., 2017). According to Piaget and Inhelder (1969), the first-hand experience of observing and handling objects and materials enables children to begin to compare them.

ECE students need to base young children's learning on the content of their everyday lives. In this way, we can ensure that the experiences being offered have connections and meaning for the child. This is because young children do not simply develop knowledge and understanding by being directed or told what to do by adults. Instead, young children are actively involved in looking, seeking, finding, feeling and exploring. This is how children receive information and make sense of it – while they are doing.

Faith (3 years, 4 months) was observed pouring sand from one cup to another. When an adult moved closer, Faith offered her a cup, saying 'tea, hot, hot!' The adult blew on the 'tea', pretending that she was cooling it down. Faith smiled at her and repeated this game for a while.

Ultimately, when children are engaged in first-hand experiences, they are active in both mind and body. When children interact and respond in their immediate environment, they are working out how to do things. Meaningful first-hand experiences provide young children with the opportunity to test out, confirm or alter their thinking and ideas about how things work and what they can do with things to make them work.

Case Study Questions and Reflection

- ECE students need to reflect on how they are supporting and building on children's first-hand experiences, existing knowledge and interests.
- How are you supporting children to make meaning from their everyday routine experiences?
- How are you using the child's awareness of symbols to support their development and understanding?

The second feature states: 'Play does not bow to pressure to conform to external rules, outcomes, targets or adult-led projects. Because of this, children keep control as they play.'

Here, ECE students are required to observe children's play with interest, be on hand to make suggestions, and act as a facilitator, enabling the children to be autonomous learners where they have choice, rather than bombarding them with a list of questions. When children are in control of their own play, they are often deeply engaged. They concentrate and take time to observe, ponder, evaluate and make sense of their experiences. Young children are very aware when adults attempt to take control of their play and will often react by retreating. It is vital that ECE students understand that children learn through play and they will need to have an abundance of opportunities where they are able to choose and control the outcomes of their own play. This happens when children are free to use resources and materials in their own way. ECE students should not try to take control of what children learn. The next observation captures an episode of children's learning in which an adult provides guidance after observing.

An adult approached James (3 years, 7 months) and Ben (3 years, 5 months) as they were looking up at the wall. She asked them, 'What are you doing?' James replied, 'We are making mud balls and throwing them on the wall and they're going splat.' The adult asked, 'Where are you getting the mud from?' James replied, 'From over there', pointing to under the tree. As it was not clean, the adult encouraged James and Ben to go and wash their hands. When they returned, the adult asked James and Ben, 'Is there any other way that you could do this?' James said, 'No... well, maybe balls', so the boys went off and collected a couple of balls and started throwing them at the wall. James said, 'It's not the same, it doesn't splat.' The adult found some soil in a bag and gave it to the boys. James and Ben put some in a bucket, added some water and then felt it with their hands. 'No, this isn't going to work,' said James, adding more water. He put his hands in again. 'No, need more water.' Ben watched as James added more, until it was wet enough to make a mud ball. James then carried the bucket to the wall and threw a mud ball against it, which went splat. James jumped up and down and did a little dance. He continued to put his hands into the mud to make more mud balls.

Case Study Questions and Reflection

- What do you think about the conversation that was recorded in this observation? Is this observation helpful in giving you a sequence of events so that you can see what James and Ben were thinking about and interested in?
- What does this observation tell you about the cognitive and physical levels of Ben and James' development?
- What does it tell you about Ben and James' friendship?
- How did James express himself?
- What does it tell you about the significance of the play?
- How often do you impose external rules on children's play?

The third feature states: 'Play is a process. It has no products. When the play ends it vanishes as quickly as it arrived.'

Children need to have the time and space to explore, discover and experiment in their own way. Play for young children is deeply serious – it is, as Froebel suggests, a child's work. ECE students will observe children running around, balancing on a wall, jumping off a step and repeating it, or riding a bike fast down a slope. In all of these activities the children are engaged in the process of play. When children are engaged in this way they are learning through doing without the external pressure of producing something. It is important that ECE students help children to express themselves and focus on the process of learning rather than the end product. Engagement in the process of play allows for children's interpretations of how they want to do things without having an end result in mind. Sometimes when students plan activities for children they may have very clear ideas about what they want the end product to look like. If a sticking activity is planned, students might expect the children to have glued materials onto the paper (the product). If a student focuses on the process instead, they may encourage the child to drizzle the glue, or explore the textures of the resource, observing the child engaging in the process of learning. In this way, students can use the process to enhance young children's learning.

> Rosie (2 years, 1 month) was observed running in circles. Later she placed her hat on the ground and ran around it until she got dizzy and fell to the floor. She then got up and repeated the process all over again.

Case Study Questions and Reflection

- Can you notice any patterns in Rosie's play? What are her strategies for learning?
- What does this observation tell you about the way in which Rosie is choosing to explore and discover her environment?
- How often do you encourage children to make props from natural materials?
- Children need opportunities to develop their symbolic play. Could you do more?

The fourth feature states: 'Children choose to play. It is intrinsically motivated. It arises spontaneously when conditions are conducive, and it is sustained as it flows.'

Intrinsic motivation means that the child is self-motivated to work towards a particular goal that they have set for themselves. Intrinsic motivation gives young children the freedom to explore and act on the things that they are interested in. Play is intrinsically motivated – we cannot force a child to play, children have to want to play. When children choose to play, they choose what game they want to play. They decide how they will play it, what they will use in their play and what part they will take. In this way, play can help children to advance in their development and learning because they do not have to follow rules and restrictions set by others, giving them the freedom to be creative. When children are intrinsically motivated, significant learning happens. ECE students need to understand the importance of children's intrinsic motivation to their levels of engagement.

> Charlotte (3 years, 5 months) had been observed over the week doing lots of mark making with chalk. She was very interested in the different bright colours. Charlotte used each colour to make lines and circles on the floor outside. It had rained a little and left a small puddle of water. Charlotte dipped the chalk in the rainwater to make it wet. As Charlotte began to make marks, she started to combine the chalks to better mix colours. She was delighted as she watched the colours get brighter and change the colour of the water.

Case Study Questions and Reflection

- How has Charlotte's play with the chalks helped to develop her creativity?
- How much are the children in your school or setting leading their own play?
- How much choice do the children have about who, what and where to play?
- Are children encouraged to do things in their own way?

The fifth feature states: 'Children rehearse their possible futures in their play. Play helps children to learn to function in advance of what they can do in the present.'

Young children are interested in what roles the adults around them do – what it is like to be a mother, father, teacher, policeman, builder, nurse or shopkeeper. Enacting these roles opens up many different possibilities for what children might become when they grow up. It also helps children to think about what it must be like to be a mother, father or doctor. ECE students will observe children rehearsing their future roles through their play. Some children will dress up and act out being a builder or traffic warden. Playing with roles in this way helps children to learn about specific tasks that a traffic warden might do, such as giving out parking tickets, and enact them in context. Children will rehearse whatever techniques they consider to be significant in the role that they have taken on. Pretend play allows children an opportunity to explore different roles and characters of the people that they experience in their everyday lives.

Aidan (2 years, 9 months) had been observed exploring with the wooden blocks and cardboard boxes in the garden. He dragged one of the boxes over to the slide and placed the cardboard box on three crates. He then put the box down and put his finger up, as if he was pushing a button. As he was pushing the button, he made an 'aaah' noise. Aidan then started to drag the cardboard box away. An adult asked, 'What are you doing?' Aidan replied, 'I am collecting rubbish and putting it in the machine.' He then went off, returned and repeated the action and the noise. The adult asked Aidan, 'What happens to the rubbish when you put it into the machine?' 'It smashes it,' Aidan replied. He spent most of the morning doing this. Later that afternoon he collected another cardboard box and the wooden blocks and put them in the machine. Later, Aidan was overheard telling another child, 'It is at the back of the dustcart, you know, where all the rubbish goes.'

Case Study Questions and Reflection

- Can you describe how this kind of play is helping Aidan to develop confidence in himself and what he might be in the future?
- What kinds of worlds do you observe that have been created by the children you work with?
- Is it just make believe or is it a mix of real and pretend?

The sixth feature states: 'Play can be solitary, and this sort of play is often very deep. Children learn who they are and how to face and deal with their ideas, feelings, relationships and physical bodies.'

Solitary play means children choosing to play alone. Sometimes children need time to play alone to develop their ideas, knowledge, feelings and understanding. As a result, solitary play is beneficial and important because it allows children to have personal space as well as offering opportunities for reflection, repetition and consideration. Solitary play also gives children the freedom to be in control of what happens, and when. ECE students should not force a child who wants to play alone to play with others. Children need time where they can be by themselves. Playing on their own gives children the freedom to do things their way, try new ideas and take risks. Ultimately, the role of the student is to observe while respecting the child's behaviour in order to be able to understand it.

Charlie (3 years, 3 months) was seen playing on his own. He threw a wooden car up onto the wall and it landed on a ledge. He tried to reach the ledge but it was too high. He found a plank of wood and tried to reach the car, but he only pushed it further back onto the ledge. He said out loud, 'It's not working, I need a long stick.' Charlie returned with the broom and at first used the handle end. 'That's not going to work,' he said, then turned the broom around and used the head to brush the car off.

Case Study Questions and Reflection

- How would you explain to a parent about the importance of children playing alone?
- Do any of your observations capture children doing things alone that they are interested in?
- Make a list of three benefits of solitary play.

The seventh feature states: 'Play has the potential to take children into a world of pretend. They imagine other worlds, creating stories of possible and impossible worlds beyond the here and now, in the past, present and future, and it transforms them into different characters.'

Pretend play is intrinsically motivated and is chosen by the child. It can be simple – a child using a block as a car – or it can be more complex, a child taking on a role in a make-believe situation. Pretend play can help children to use and develop their imagination in creative and abstract ways. In many respects, pretend play is a child's way of not just recalling a past experience but also of developing their understanding about the world that they live in. When children are engaged in pretend play in which they act out a role, they are beginning to understand what people do in different roles and situations.

Pretend play is important for children, as it enables them to understand and cope with their experiences. Children play out their experiences before they can talk. ECE students can help children by giving them time to play and by supporting and encouraging this kind of play.

> Kiyan (3 years) was playing with large wooden blocks in the garden. He laid one block on the ground and then started to build around it with taller blocks. He spent some time adjusting the blocks until he was happy with their position. Kiyan then put four much longer blocks around the taller blocks and climbed inside. An adult approached and asked what he had made. Kiyan replied that it was a jail and he was in jail. Kiyan would not let any of the other children into the jail. He told the adult that he did not want them in there. After a short while Kiyan extended the structure and built more walls around the edge. The adult asked him if he was making his jail bigger. He said, 'No, it's a boat.' He would not let other children inside his boat. He docked his boat and then said he needed a sail so that he could move.

Case Study Questions and Reflection

- Are your observations capturing children representing things symbolically?
- Do your observations capture children as complex symbol users?
- Can you see what knowledge and understanding Kiyan has about what makes a boat sail?
- How could you use this information to support his understanding?
- Do you reflect on how much symbolic knowledge children are using as they play and explore?

The eighth feature states: 'Children and/or adults can play together, in parallel (companionship play), associatively or co-operatively in pairs or groups.'

Co-operative play is social play. It encourages children to play together and helps them to learn about social skills and getting along with others, as well as encouraging them to share and take turns.

> Jada (3 years, 6 months) and Robyn (3 years, 8 months) were observed playing together in a mud 'kitchen'. They prepared the food using stones, shells and pebbles and then set the table. Jada served the food and Robyn poured out the water. The girls were overheard planning what and how they would play. Jada said, 'Let's go to the shops to buy some ice cream before we go to the park. Let's take the car, I can drive.'

Case Study Questions and Reflection

- Do your observations capture how pretend play helps children to communicate?
- Are you observing how children express their ideas and feelings?
- Think about your last observation in which you saw children pretending as they played. What do you think was important to them?
- How do you think that this kind of play helps to develop the whole child?

The ninth feature states: 'Play can be initiated by a child or an adult, but adults need to bear in mind that every player has his or her own personal play agenda (of which he or she may be unaware) and respect this by not insisting that the adult agenda dominates the play.'

ECE students will need to know how and when to intervene in children's play, so that it remains child-led (Fisher, 2016). This means that students need to be able to recognise and respect the agency and motivation behind the play of individual children.

An adult set up the role play area into a shop and wanted the children to practise their use of number skills. The children did not want to play shops – instead they wanted to make face masks, put on hand sanitiser and play games about queuing and social distancing. One child wanted to make the coronavirus. The adult took the children's play ideas seriously and went along with them. She supported the play by suggesting that the children could also make signs showing two metres distance and signs to let shoppers know how many people were allowed in the store. In this way, the adult recognises and respects the children's agency and motivation.

Case Study Questions and Reflection

- What was important for you in this observation? What would you have written down? What did you find interesting?
- How seriously do you take children's pretend play on a scale of one to ten? (Ten being very seriously.)
- Can you think about a time when children invited you to join in their play? Did you take their ideas and questions seriously?
- Can you think about a time when you may have joined in play without being invited? In this situation, were you aware of the children's personal agenda?
- Do your observations capture children leading their own interests in play which they are free to explore?
- Do you feel confident intervening in children's play?

- Can you think of a time that you were able to intervene in child-initiated play sensitively?
- Do your observations capture the motivations behind children's actions?

The tenth feature states: 'Children's free-flow play is characterised by deep concentration, and it is difficult to distract them from their learning. Children at play wallow in their learning.'

Young children need to have uninterrupted time to play so that they can explore the things that interest them (Gopnik, Meltzoff and Kuhl, 1999). If children are not interested in what they are doing it can be difficult for them to concentrate.

While on a trip to the zoo, Harry (3 years) was not interested in looking at the elephants. He was much more interested in studying a passing wheelchair. Harry could not take his eyes off the chair. He insisted that his mother followed the chair so that he could see how it moved. When he got home, Harry tipped his pushchair on its side and started to spin the wheels again and again. Later in the week, Harry found a small world figure of a little girl in a wheelchair. He spent a long time walking around with it. He then found an adult figure to place behind the wheelchair to push the little girl around.

Case Study Questions and Reflection

- How are your observations of play capturing children's mental development?
- How are children making their ideas visible in your observations?
- Can you see any links and/or connections between how Harry is exploring his ideas, feelings and experiences?

The eleventh feature states: 'In play, children try out their most recent learning, mastery, competencies and skills, and consolidate them. They use their technical prowess and confidently apply their learning.'

This means that children will demonstrate what they know and can do in their play. When ECE students observe children at play they will notice that children will apply their previous learning to it. As Froebel says:

The mind grows by self-revelation. In play the child ascertains what he can do, discovers his possibilities of will and thought by exerting his power spontaneously. In work he follows a task prescribed for him by another and doesn't reveal his own proclivities and inclinations; but another's. In play he reveals his own original power. (1887: 54–5)

This means that, in play, children will apply their recent learning.

Tia (3 years, 11 months) was seen exploring the tessellation shapes. She spent some time just looking at them. After a while, Tia began to select the hexagons from the middle of the pile and, one by one, she placed them around the outside of another hexagon, pushing the shapes together to form a pattern with no gaps. At one point there was a tiny gap, so she added a diamond shape which brought the pattern together. When she ran out of diamond shapes, she found two triangles which she put together to make a diamond and placed it in the gap of the hexagonal shapes.

Case Study Questions and Reflection

• Can you see how Tia was able to use what she knew in her play?
• Do your observations capture children experimenting and finding things out for themselves?
• How do you use your observations to build on what children already know and can do?
• Do you collect observations of children applying what they know to their play?
• This observation of Tia shows clearly how play and development are connected.

The twelfth feature states: 'Children at play co-ordinate their ideas and feelings and make sense of relationships with family, friends and culture. Play is an integrating mechanism that allows flexible, adaptive, imaginative and innovative behaviour. Play makes children into whole people, able to keep balancing their lives in a fast-changing world.'

In play, children co-ordinate their ideas, thoughts and feelings, as well as their physical bodies. They are able to make sense of their social relationships and their sense of themselves within the world around them. Ultimately, play is a child's main way of recalling their experiences. The process enables children to use their play in creative and imaginative ways. As play develops, children are able to come up with new ideas and ways of doing things in order to keep their play going. It is important to keep in mind that, in order for a child to use what they have seen in their play, they need to make it part of themselves. They have to put it together and understand it in some way.

Alex (3 years, 2 months) was observed playing with a fire station on the play mat. He then went off and came back with a fire engine and three police officer figures, saying that they were firemen. He pushed the truck around the road looking for a fire. He spent some time clearing trees that were blocking the road. When he finally reached the fire, he made a 'sssssshhhh' noise, like the water from a hose. He then kept this going, looking for other fires to put out.

Case Study Questions and Reflection

- Are your observations capturing play that flows?
- Do your observations capture how children use play to bring their ideas and feelings together?
- How closely are you observing children?
- Observation is vital if ECE students are to understand and interpret children's play.

Observation and the 12 Features

Play for children is an important part of being human and alive – they need to play and try out ideas (Froebel, 1887). Students' observations should always emanate from children being actively involved in the experience. The 12 features seek to highlight the central importance of play. Through studying them and being aware of them, ECE students can gain a deeper knowledge and understanding about the children they work with. It is the pedagogical responsibility of the ECE student to gather observational information that informs how they support and plan for individual children's development, interests, communication and learning styles. ECE students' observations need to identify and note significant learning so that they can plan ways to nourish and enrich the child's experience. Students need to learn to act on what they observe, using observational information to make appropriate assessments of where children are in their development and learning, in order to support them sensitively. In 1840, Froebel considered observations to be a fundamental part of practice and that play was a 'child's work'. He understood the importance of allowing children the freedom to learn new things for themselves and not to discourage them from doing something, even if the adult thought it might not be safe, such as climbing trees. Today's research indicates that, in the most effective schools and settings, observation is acknowledged as a crucial aspect of the educator's role and as such is given appropriate status in relation to everyday practice. Educators are not technicians, filling in forms, pulling levers and pressing buttons to produce regulated approved end products. Instead, they are observing and gathering information from all sorts of sources, including intuition about children, in order to make the most accurate assessment or judgement that they can about what children know and what children don't know (Drummond, 1993).

Reflection

Students need to:

- Recognise that observing the 12 features of play will give them specific information about children's development and understanding.

- Regularly take time out to observe and listen to what children are saying and doing.
- Always reflect on how meaningful the experience that you are offering children is.

Conclusion

The 12 features of play highlight key indicators that we need to pay attention to. Observing the way that play co-ordinates development and learning includes how we see children make use of first-hand experiences, keep control in the way they make rules, follow their own play agenda, and not become easily distracted. They create pretend play scenarios, make props, try out ideas and feelings and make sense of their lives, choosing when and how to play alone, or with other children or adults (Bruce, 1991 and 2019).

The observations that ECE students make of toddlers and young children will capture the different ways in which children play. When ECE students understand and recognise what they see children doing, they are in a great position to support and extend children's learning. In the next chapter, we will explore schemas and why children like to do things again and again.

References

Bruce, T. (1991) *Time to Play in Early Childhood Education*. London: Hodder & Stoughton.

Bruce, T. (2015) *Early Childhood Education* (5th edn). London: Hodder & Stoughton.

Bruce, T. (2019) *Educating Young Children: A Lifetime Journey into a Froebelian Approach. The Selected Works of Tina Bruce*. London: Routledge.

Drummond, M.J. (1993) *Assessing Children's Learning*. London: David Fulton.

Fisher, J. (2016) *Interacting or Interfering? Improving Interactions in the Early Years*. Maidenhead: Open University Press.

Froebel, F. (1887) *The Education of Man*. New York: Appleton.

Gopnik, A., Meltzoff, A.N. and Kuhl, P.K. (1999) *The Scientist in the Crib: Mind, Brains, and How Children Learn*. New York, NY: William Morrow & Company.

Piaget, J. and Inhelder, B. (1969) *The Psychology of the Child*. New York: Basic Books.

Zosh, J.M., Hopkins, E.J., Jensen, H., Liu, C., Neale, D., Hirsh-Pasek, K., Solis, S.L. and Whitebread, D. (2017) 'Learning Through Play: A Review of the Evidence'. *LEGO Foundation*.

5
SCHEMAS

Introduction

Babies, toddlers and young children go through a specific and very important stage of development and learning called schemas. Schemas are biological and appear in babies and children throughout the world. Athey (1990: 37) defines a schema as 'a pattern of repeatable behaviour into which experiences are assimilated and that are gradually co-ordinated. Co-ordinations lead to higher-level and more powerful schemas'.

Put simply, schemas are repeated actions that young children try out on the things that they encounter in their environment. Schemas are human and cut across race, gender and culture. They are dependent upon children's first-hand experiences, as well as the cultural context in which they grow up. Schemas are also sociocultural – that is, the people, children, adults and culture that the child grows up with influences that child's biological path. As young children gain more opportunities to repeat activities, they begin to demonstrate their knowledge of schemas in many different ways.

For example, a child may repeatedly hide objects in the sand and in boxes with lids. This can not only lead to them exploring concepts of object permanence (that things exist even though they are out of sight) but it can also help to develop their memory about where they have put things. Similarly, joining things together can help children to understand connectivity and sequences. As schemas develop they become more and more complex and students may observe children exploring a range of schematic concepts. The co-ordination aspect of the schema is important as it helps to improve the child's developing skills. This then leads to more powerful schemas.

A number of repetitive actions are seen from a very early age. They include:

- Tracking
- Gazing

- Vertical and horizontal movement
- Circular movements
- Enveloping or containing
- Dynamic vertical movements – up and down
- Dynamic horizontal movements – back and forth and side to side
- Dynamic circular movements – round and rotation
- Going over and under

Knowledge of schemas will help students to understand why a child might hide objects in the sand or tie rope across furniture. Schemas are a useful tool for observing, assessing and planning for children's development. Students need to be able to recognise the schematic pattern in what the children do so that they can then support or extend children's learning. This means that if we observe a child in a variety of different activities – connecting carriages, tracks, construction toys and rope – we can support the child with language by describing what they are doing and we will understand the need to make sure that the physical environment provides the child with a range of materials to use in connecting.

Schemas are Part of Piagetian Theory

Jean Piaget (1896–1980) was interested in how children gain knowledge, specifically their intellectual development. He recognises that for children to acquire knowledge they must first have experience with people, objects and the environment using all of their senses. He believes that repetition is a powerful tool for learning because it allows children to perceive and predict (Piaget and Inhelder, 1956).

Children will often be observed playing the same game again and again. In fact, they will play out events that they have experienced in their everyday lives – putting baby to bed, playing mummies and daddies, going shopping. It is true to say that a great deal of play by babies, toddlers and young children appears to be repetitive and related to their everyday lives. It is important that ECE students understand that the constant repetition helps children to become more familiar with their everyday experiences and be able to recall and internalise events. Repeating actions helps children to be able to recall what they know, even when they do not yet have language. Piaget and Inhelder (1956) define schemas as Assimilation, Adaptation and Accommodation.

Assimilation is where children are constantly taking in and understanding new experiences. For example, John (3 years, 9 months) has had some magnetic shape tiles (triangle, square and rectangle) for about 18 months. In that time, he has explored them – stacking, building towers, tessellating, exploring properties and partitioning shapes. All that he has learned has been embedding and assimilating in his mind. He said to his mum, 'I'm putting up Christmas decorations.' He made the trees, selecting the colours and the patterns. His repetition allows him to build on his new experiences which, in turn, support his symbolic play. This is where John is exploring and applying what he has learned in a different context. Assimilation is the repeated process that takes place over time and allows the child to embed and integrate new learning, making the experience part of themselves and their thinking.

Adaptation relates to how the experience of stacking, building towers, tesselating, exploring properties and partitioning shapes leads John to new ways of thinking that are rooted in previous discoveries. In this way, John can be seen to be organising, analysing, interpreting and re-interpreting by linking to his first-hand experiences. He now has the confidence to move from exploring to develop his thinking by assuming what he has learned to be a rule of how things behave.

Accommodation is where children need repeated experiences in order to take in learning. If an experience has not been accommodated it cannot become part of the child. Repetition helps children to accommodate new experiences and supports additional experiences to become accommodated. This is where John's learning has become internalised and part of the structure of his thinking.

How Do Schemas Develop?

The *Early Years Foundation Stage* defines schemas as 'patterns of repeated behaviour in children'. It says:

> Children often have a very strong drive to repeat actions such as moving things from one place to another, covering things up and putting things into containers, moving in circles or throwing things. These patterns can often be observed running through their play and will vary between one child and another. If practitioners build on these interests, powerful learning can take place. (2006: 134)

Schemas develop through first-hand experience and are related to brain development (Shore, 1997). In recent years, neuroscientists have discovered that babies, toddlers and young children need to do things in a number of different ways – and at least 400 times – before connections are made in the developing brain. According to the Welsh Government (2021: 54), 'Schemas can support children to express their developing ideas and thoughts through their exploratory play. The repetitive actions of schematic play allow children to construct meaning in what they are doing.'

In the first few years of life, a baby's brain is rapidly developing with millions of connections being formed every second. Every interaction the baby has with people or objects has a direct impact on how these connections develop. Initially, babies' responses are involuntary actions and movements. However, once they start to become more mobile and experienced, they are able to combine their sensory skills, ability to filter information and their perception. For example, they begin to repeat their actions deliberately, purposefully and thoughtfully and will use their senses, attention and perception to help them to understand their immediate world. They will be observed using movement and all of their senses to look at, seek, find, feel and investigate things around them. When we observe the ways in which babies, toddlers and young children interact with people, objects and the environment we notice these repeated patterns in their behaviour. Birth to 5 Matters (2021: 81) encourages educators to 'Notice a child who moves repetitively in a particular way e.g. spinning around, flapping hands or using a throwing action'.

Why Do Schemas Matter?

According to the Welsh Government,

> Schemas can play a key role in laying the foundations for future mathematical and scientific understanding; they provide physical opportunities to fully understand language concepts and encourage problem-solving and creative thinking. Children's exploratory drive to find out how and why things happen strengthens their neural pathways making it easier for children to make connections in learning, test out their emergent thinking and make choices and decisions. Failing to provide opportunities for children to fully embrace and explore their schemas may be detrimental to their sense of agency. (2021: 54)

Through their repeated actions, young children reveal their thinking to us long before they can even talk or understand what is being said to them. By repeating simple actions such as dropping or throwing things, children begin to understand the properties of materials. For example, a feather will flutter and flow through the air while a stone is heavier and will fall to the ground. This gradual process of repeating experiences and gathering information leads to children acquiring knowledge and understanding particular concepts – this is what Athey (1990) means by more powerful schemas. These early concepts are only just beginning to be explored.

It is worthwhile pointing out that children will use more than one schema, that the actions in one schema may be seen in another and that there is an element of crossover. Bruce (1996) reminds us that 'schemas are patterns of linked behaviours which the child can generalise and use in a whole variety of situations. It is best to think of schemas as a cluster of pieces which fit together'. These clusters develop further into abstract concepts.

Schemas help children to create mental maps. If children cannot remember what they have done, they have not learnt anything – that is why repetition is key for the development of memory. The Scottish Government's *Building the Ambition* echoes this idea and states that schemas are

> patterns of repeated behaviour which can often be noticed in young children's play. The skilled practitioner is able to recognise that these distinct patterns of behaviour are meaningful and accommodate opportunities for individual children. For example, children carrying all the bricks from one place to another in a bag; or the sand from the tray to the home corner or pushing a doll around in a pram. This repeated behaviour could be described as Transporting – one of the examples of schematic play. It is important to be aware that occasional actions and fleeting interests are not schemas. (2014: 40)

A child's schema will be evident across a range of different situations. It is important for a practitioner to understand that a child is not being disruptive when engaged in schematic play but be able to recognise this as early learning and help to support the child by offering opportunities to test out their thinking.

Children will also need opportunities to explore so that they can turn their experiences into useable knowledge. Schemas help children to turn their experiences into know-how. Therefore, children will need many experiences in a variety of situations to understand the different properties of a feather and a leaf. Through schematic play, children engage in and encounter many concepts in their own way at their own pace. Children are constantly absorbing new information and experiences which they will internalise so that they can build on these new experiences and accommodate them.

The Scottish Government's *Realising the Ambition* reminds us that

> spending time reflecting on observations enables us to consider what children are interested in or curious about, what ideas they are exploring, or skills they are developing. It may be that, for some children, the observations give an insight into the schemas children are engaging in or their dispositions for learning. (2020: 66)

ECE students can help children, either individually or in groups, to develop their understanding by recognising schemas and providing meaningful resources to support them. Observing schemas and using them as the basis for supporting and extending children's holistic development and learning is fundamental. If we do not get this stage right, where the process of doing things repeatedly is nurtured, the child's further development will be hampered. It is vital that ECE students understand how a child shows their thinking through schemas and what concepts a child might be exploring. This is why it is so important that ECE students need to be able to recognise this as early learning and support the child by offering opportunities to test out their thinking.

Piaget developed an elaborate structure to outline how children acquire knowledge. Within this structure he further highlights the need for sensory integration and primitive and conscious symbolic play. Piaget believed that, as babies develop and grow, schemas will be seen operating in four different ways – sensory and movement development; symbolic representation; functional dependency; and abstract thought.

Sensory and Movement Development

Before babies are able to explore and play, they must first combine their movement and manipulation skills. Young children will be observed combining movement with the information they gather through their senses (what they see, hear, touch, taste and smell). Babies will filter this information and use their perception to analyse, organise, interpret and reinterpret it. When we observe a baby or toddlers, we may notice just how much questioning, examining and weighing up is expressed in their eyes (Froebel, 1886).

Babies and toddlers have a sensory need to focus their eyes on objects that are new and of interest, for example, examining coloured and shining things. Sometimes children do things solely for physical enjoyment of the experience, the feeling of running back and forth, turning around and around, climbing up and down on furniture, jumping and throwing – or they may just want to watch glue dripping from a brush. What's important at this stage is the feel of the sand, water, dough or clay on the child's hands, or watching the glue drizzle onto paper. The feeling of the materials is of interest to infants and young children, not producing a glued product. The process of doing needs to be experienced fully and thoroughly without being rushed. Meade and Cubey (2008: 6) provide a useful example – 'Alastair (3 years, 9 months), on a visit to the Science Museum, could not be moved from a mechanical model of a man rotating a handle, which turned a large wooden screw in order to winch water from the well.'

Learning develops from the child's sensory memory of their interactions with the world. Repetitive movements aid their memory, enabling them to remember intentional actions as opposed to their early reflex responses. Schemas can be described as non-verbal memories of an experience. When we see children using a repeated action to explore and discover its effect on things, they are demonstrating their thinking through action. The following observations give some examples.

William (2 years) was observed playing with the water tray over several weeks. He repeatedly used a jug to scoop the water into a bucket.

Day after day, Marissa (21 months) would be seen at the sink turning the tap on and watching the running water. She would then pull the plug out, run more water and watch it go down the plug hole.

Samuel (15 months) was observed watching dry sand flow through his fingers.

Children will repeat these sensory movements and actions for the pure physical sensation of the experience – the feel of the water as it runs through their fingers, or the sight of the flowing sand. On these occasions children are interested in doing, experimenting and exploring with their senses.

Molly Davies (2003: 61) was interested in how children move and think and describes how movement 'permeates the complex process of early growth and development unifying the physical, cognitive, emotional and social aspects of life'. Davies argues that sometimes children choose movement for its own sake and use it expressively, such as spinning for the joy of it, or moving to music. Children also respond to experience with movement, for example, waves breaking on the sand, or a car taking a bend at speed. The experience of movement and moving objects often blurs with representational/expressive movement (for example, a child dragging chairs into a line and calling them a train merges with the pleasure of climbing on and off them).

According to Gerhardt (1973: 120), 'Body movement is the foundation of thought. It derives from and contributes to sensory perception, imagery and thought. Each human being organises his/her experiences to his/her own patterns.' This means that a child's movements reflect their individual experiences as well as the shared meanings of a particular culture, for example, moving to music. Personal style is important too – one child may express happiness in exuberant movement and another through quiet stillness. Therefore, you cannot say a specific movement reflects a particular feeling.

Symbolic Representation

Once children are walking and talking, they will repeatedly pretend to do familiar actions, such as putting baby to bed or having dinner. By their first year, children will have learned a great deal about going to bed and eating, so they can apply this information to their play. Students will observe children exploring specific schemas symbolically.

Meade and Cubey (2008: 6) provide a symbolic example – 'Alastair (3 years, 9 months) [made] a car with wheels. He made the wheels go round and said, "Look, they go round". He then pointed to square shapes on top (seats) and said, "And they go round". He had been absorbed by the typist's [swivel] chair.'

It is important that toddlers and young children are able to practise what they know about going to bed and eating in a literal way. This means that children will need real dolls and beds and everyday household materials to play with. Through their play, children will be observed using things that are similar to the actual object – for example, a child might use a large paint brush to sweep the floor or a smaller paint brush to paint their nails.

As children gain more real first-hand experience, their play moves from literal, real and concrete to symbolic play. Here the child may use a stick to stand in for a baby and a tin may represent the bed. This is an important milestone in development and learning – when a child is able to make one thing represent something else.

Children will have many different ways of repeating a particular schema within the context of symbolic representation. For example, a child who is interested in the Trajectory or Transporting schema may line up sticks pretending that they are parked cars. Students need to understand the significance of when a child realises that they can use objects to symbolically carry meaning because this is the child's way of making their thinking visible. This kind of play not only supports children's use of symbols, helping to develop their imaginary and abstract ideas, but also links to the things that they talk about in their play.

John Matthews' work looks at actions being given meaning through early mark making (the beginning of visual representation). He notes that babies are interested in movement rather than form or colour. He refers to the work of Colwyn Trevarthen (1999–2000), where babies control and synchronise their own rhythmical patterns with their caregiver and suggests that the timing, tempo and cadence of these become the structure for later play, construction, drawing and painting. Matthews (2002: 31) says, 'Early painting and drawing are a dialogue between what the child wants to do and what appears on the paper.' He adds that, in a process similar to language acquisition, children explore the pattern and structure of their drawings and the actions which make them. This is where the child is also combining dynamic action schemas with figurative (image) schemas in the following sequence of development:

- There are three mark-making gestures – vertical arc (one month), horizontal arc (three months) and push-pull (four months) which emerge and are given particular meaning within a social context.
- Between one and two years children begin to realise that movements make marks and different movements make different marks. They go on to separate out and classify lines and actions. From 18 months, points in space and continuous rotations develop. The *Aistear: the Early Childhood Curriculum Framework* (2009: 58) notes that the supportive adult should 'give support to babies to try new things and also to practise and repeat activities'.

Matthews (2002) also notes that from two years children combine movement and marks (travelling zigzags and loops). Throughout this process, they practise and repeat what they know and imbue their marks with emotional and representational possibilities. Children create their own drawing rules and use them to make new combinations which change.

- By three to four years old children start to represent objects and their movement. This is linked to language acquisition as the pictures are associated with a spoken narrative.
- They go on to explore the difference between symbols (which capture something of the shape of the object) and signs (letters, numbers and words) whose shapes are arbitrary and conventional. They use drawing to sort out the difference between how signs and symbols work.

Functional Dependency

Functional dependency requires children to have an understanding of the beginning and the end state, but also the steps in between. This is where a child will do one thing to make something else happen. For example, a child might pretend to use keys to get into the house or buy a ticket to board a train or plane or know that the blocks are going to fall over if they put another block on top. In this way, children begin to reveal their understanding about cause and effect relationships. According to Bruce, Louis and McCall (2015), during this stage we begin to see the early development of cause and effect relationships emerging.

Meade and Cubey (2008: 7) provide observations of Alastair 12 months later.

Alastair (4 years, 9 months), following a visit to the railway, worked with Jack (4 years, 9 months). They made a level crossing. They set up the railway track, intersected with a road [grid schema]. They closed the level-crossing by 'rotating' them so that they closed off the road.... They made the train go along the tracks. They 'rotated' the gates back again, and made the cars move across the railway line.

Cause and effect for children is about developing an understanding of what might happen. For example, a child might be interested in how a toy works and they may take it apart in order to understand its cause and effect functions. Similarly, a child might be interested in finding out what makes the bicycle wheels go round. This is thinking at its highest level, when children understand that if they do one thing, they can make something else happen.

Transforming relates to children making discoveries in their explorations. It is sometimes referred to as a schema, but it's not – it comes about as a result of children engaging in schematic play. Children may become absorbed by the ability to change things, observing what happens when they mix paints, or cook, cut or melt them. Cause and effect are the beginning of scientific exploration.

Example 1 – Sophia (3 years, 1 month) was observed warming her hands on the radiator, then melting a piece of chocolate in her hands.

   Example 2 – Jessie (3 years) was observed moving her boat and other floating objects in the water tray. She held her boat down and started to pour water over it to make it sink. Over the next few weeks, she discovered that, by repeatedly pouring water from one container into another, containers full of water will stand on the bottom too.

   Example 3 – Bobby (3 years) insisted on wearing his green jacket to the park on a beautiful summer day because it helped him to go faster on the slide.

Abstract Thought

Meade and Cubey provide us with one of their earlier observations of Alastair which demonstrates that development is not linear but proceeds in a web of numerous strands, as also noted by Evangelou et al. (2009).

> Alastair (3 years, 6 months) noted the effect on wet clothes of 'turning' the handle of a mangle. His mother encouraged him by suggesting he reversed the direction... [Later], Alastair started a conversation with his father about a fishing rod. He said, "You know a fishing rod? When you throw it out [he made a gesture of casting a line] the string goes right out." His mother asked him what happens when you reverse the rotation of the handle. Alastair said, "The line gets shorter." (Meade and Cubey, 2008: 7)

Abstract thought is when children tell us about things, concepts and ideas that they have experienced. For example, Alice (4 years, 5 months) was fascinated with making things. Over several months she was observed making different sizes of umbrellas from recycled materials. Using a large egg box and a kitchen roll tube, Alice carefully centred the tube in the middle and attached it with tape. She then decorated it with corks, making sure that there were an equal number hanging from each side. In spite of this, the umbrella would not stay upright. When the adult asked Alice if it was balanced, she replied, "No", without examining it. Because Alice had been exploring this for several months, she knew it was not the same. Later, without the umbrella being present, Alice explained that one of the corks was a different size to the others and that is why it was not balanced. Abstract thought helps children to make clear what they do and do not understand.

Schemas can be dynamic (movements) or figurative (capturing a static movement in graphics, drawings and mark making – symbolic) (Athey, 1990). For example, with the Enveloping schema, children may dynamically fill and empty buckets. With the figurative form, a child might draw the sand inside the sand pit. For example, in his painting, Toby formed dabs, spots and dots and an enclosed line. He then covered it up with paint. He labelled this as his 'sand pit'. These behaviours are connected – they help children to explore and learn how things work. By observing both the dynamic and figurative forms of schemas, ECE students can begin to better understand children's motivations to do particular things and the types of activities that they concentrate on and become deeply involved in. Our observations of children will help us to see the connections and complexities involved in their play, facilitating a deeper understanding of the process by which individual children learn from schemas (Louis et al., 2012).

Reflection

- Are you observing babies and young children making choices and decisions about what they play with?
- Are your observations capturing children concentrating on their interests and being deeply involved?
- Do you offer resources that children can jump on or over, kick a ball through, balance on, climb on and get into and under?
- Are there continuously available resources and natural materials for children to handle and transport freely?
- Are all adults knowledgeable and confident about the developing concept behind particular schemas?

Conclusion

It is important not to discourage repetition but to value both the dynamic and figurative form of schemas. Together they give us insight, not just into the child's outer expression but also their inner thoughts and understanding. ECE students need to consider what schemas are telling them about children's thinking and developing concepts. They must reflect on their observations so that they can really see what children are interested in or intrigued by, what ideas they are incubating, and what skills they are developing. According to Louis:

> Although basic schemas are found in every human in every part of the world – in the same way as vision, hearing, touch and movement are present, unless there is damage – there are fascinating variations in the way in which they present, according to cultural contexts and individual interests which emphasise some schemas more than others. (2021: 1)

Schemas are part of our biological development but also part of our social and cultural experiences. This includes how adults can provide an appropriate curriculum that fits the biological form of children's schemas and supports them to use their schematic knowledge in a number of different ways.

Schemas are sometimes characterised as a type of play which is essentially unimportant, trivial and lacking in any serious goal – that children do it because they are naughty or bored. On the contrary, it is important for ECE students to understand that the child is revealing their thinking. ECE students need to be able to recognise what concepts or ideas children might be exploring and find meaningful ways to support them. Ultimately, schemas help students to reflect on how to tune into individual children's interest and needs.

References

Athey, C. (1990) *Extending Thought in Young Children: A Parent-Teacher Partnership*. London: Paul Chapman Publishing.

Bruce, T. (1996) *Helping Young Children to Play*. London: Hodder & Stoughton.

Bruce, T., Louis, S. and McCall, G. (2015) *Observing Young Children*. London: Sage.

Davies, M. (2003) *Movement and Dance in Early Childhood* (2nd edn). London: Paul Chapman Publishing.

Early Education (2021) *Birth to 5 Matters: Non-statutory Guidance for the Early Years Foundation Stage; Guidance by the sector for the sector*. St Albans: Early Education.

Early Years Foundation Stage (EYFS) (2006) *Consultation Document*. London: DfES.

Evangelou, M., Sylva, K., Kyriacou, M., Wild, M. and Glenny, G. (2009) *Early Years Learning and Development Literature Review Research Report Number DCSF-RR176*. London: Department for Children, Schools and Families.

Froebel, F. (1886) *Mother's Songs, Games and Stories*. Rendered in English by Lord, F. and Lord, E. London: William Rice.

Gerhardt, L. (1973) *Moving and Knowing: The Young Child Orients Himself in Space*. Englewood Cliffs, NJ: Prentice-Hall.

Louis, S. (2021) 'What are schemas? Aren't they just what all children do?' *That Nursery Life* (TNL).

Louis, S., Beswick, C., Magraw, L. and Hayes, L. (2012) *Understanding Schemas in Young Children: Again! Again!* (Edited by S. Featherstone). London: Featherstone.

Matthews, J. (2002) *Helping Children to Draw and Paint in Early Childhood*. London: Paul Chapman Publishing.

Meade, A. and Cubey, P. (2008) *Thinking Children: Learning about Schemas*. New Zealand Council for Educational Research and Institute for Early Childhood Studies, Wellington College of Education/Victoria University of Wellington.

National Council for Curriculum and Assessment (NCCA) (2009) *Aistear: The Early Childhood Curriculum Framework*. Dublin: National Council for Curriculum and Assessment.

Piaget, J. and Inhelder, B. (1956) *The Child's Conception of Space*. London: Routledge & Kegan Paul.

The Scottish Government (2014) *Building the Ambition: National Practice Guidance on Early Learning and Childcare Children and Young People (Scotland)*. Edinburgh: The Scottish Government.

The Scottish Government (2020) *Realising the Ambition: National Practice Guidance for Early Years in Scotland*. Edinburgh: The Scottish Government.

Shore, R. (1997) *Rethinking the Brain: New Insights into Early Development*. New York: Families and Work Institute.

Trevarthen, C. (1999–2000) 'Musicality and the intrinsic motive pulse: Evidence from human psychobiology and infant communication'. Special issue of *Music Scientiae, Rhythm, Musical Narrative and Origins of Human Communication*. pp. 156–99.

The Welsh Government (2021) *A Curriculum for Funded Non-Maintained Nursery Settings* (Consultation Document). Cardiff: The Welsh Government.

6
OBSERVING AND IDENTIFYING SCHEMAS

Introduction

The Welsh Government (2021: 54) reminds ECE students that, 'Some children have a very strong drive to repeat actions such as lining objects up, moving things from place to place, filling and emptying containers, covering things, or throwing them.'

Many different forms of biological schemas have been identified by Athey (1990) – but here we will focus on:

- Trajectory
- Enclosure
- Enveloping
- Transporting
- Rotation
- Connecting
- Positioning
- Topological

Students can regard each one as a family 'head' which has several related schemas. The Welsh Government says:

Some children may be observed with one very clear schema; while others may display a number of schemas called clusters. Schemas may change over time, for example, a child may experiment with a particular schema such as enveloping themselves in blankets or scarfs before moving onto enveloping objects of varying sizes with fabric or paint. As soon as children integrate new learning into existing schema they adjust their current thinking to accommodate these new experiences. (2021: 54)

This means that whatever a child does schematically to themselves, they also do with their playthings. This is why schemas are so important to observe and understand.

Trajectory

The Trajectory schema is one of the best known. Babies, toddlers and young children display this schema when they track things with their eyes, kick, pull, push, reach out and retract. The Trajectory schema relates to an exploration of either vertical or horizontal lines, up and down movements, or back and forth. Young children are often interested in how things move or fly through the air and toddlers are well known for throwing things from their highchair and climbing on objects. Dynamically, a child may be fascinated with dropping objects, tracking with their eyes, climbing, stepping up and down, throwing, jumping and moving through space, as well as 'flying' things like balls, aeroplanes, rockets, catapults and frisbees. Figuratively, they may put vertical or horizonal lines in constructions, collages, paintings and drawings. Children learn in this way about height through exploring up and down as well as developing understanding about space, speed and distance and incremental sequences, such as higher and lower.

Martha (18 months) was observed climbing on a small tree. She tested a number of different ways to grip the tree trunk with her hands, then she explored her balance. This helped her to work out that she needed to transfer her weight from her feet to her arms. She thoughtfully positioned her hands and feet and pulled her body up the trunk of the tree. Martha later used a stick and her finger to draw vertical lines of different sizes in the soil.

Jake and Josh (both 4 years) were seen stacking crates, encouraging each other to put another one on top until they fell over. Josh later made vertical marks with a stick in the sand.

Rio (9 months) was observed throwing blocks in different directions and across the room.

Trajectories later develop to become more co-ordinated and rather sophisticated. These are some examples:

Clashing trajectory is where two trajectories meet. Dynamically, some children may bite or pinch, bang toys together, or throw and crash toys against walls or furniture or off the ground. Figuratively, children start to draw strips or a series of lines (horizontal or vertical). Their paintings and drawings are ordered with parallel lines.

Amanda (3 years, 4 months) went on an underground train for the first time. Afterwards she was observed opening and closing her knees, pretending to be the doors of the Tube train. In her drawings she drew several parallel lines, close together and far apart.

John (3 years, 8 months) had found a pair of scissors. The adult gave him some paper, which he cut up. He spent some time stapling the paper.

Jacob (4 years) was observed picking up stones using tweezers. He then crashed cars into the wall over and over again.

Crosses or Grids

Once children have explored horizontal and vertical trajectories separately, the two are often co-ordinated to form crosses and grids. This helps children to develop a fuller understanding of direction, up and down and across. Dynamically, some children show an interest in creating symmetrical square and rectangular grids in their building, models and construction play. Figuratively, children may explore a range of shapes and patterns in their drawings.

Abbey (5 years) was observed over several weeks arranging flat lollipop sticks into horizontal and vertical positions which she later taped onto paper. She later drew a similar design on the chalkboard.

Mason (4 years, 3 months) was observed mark making. He combined straight and curved lines and explained it was snakes and ladders. He was later noticed closely studying an illustration in a book of snakes and ladders.

Harry (5 years) was observed constructing a symmetrical square grid using blocks. He then drew several symmetrical square and rectangular grids.

Obliques

This schema usually appears later. Children may show an interest in diagonal lines or zigzags, with zigzags often followed by diagonals, and may be fascinated by sloping lines. Dynamically, children will construct slopes, ramps, slides and roofs. Figuratively, diagonal lines and zigzags are seen in their paintings and drawings.

Daniel (3 years, 5 months) used a selection of blocks and planks to make roads which sloped to form diagonals. Daniel was overheard saying, 'This road is getting too straight, we need to have a slope.' Several days later, he painted a picture of a 'saw' with a serrated blade and a diagonal handle.

Jon (2 years, 8 months) was observed singing to himself and opening and closing his hands at the same time. He then drew zigzags and said they were 'teeth'.

Pat (5 years, 2 months) used guttering and planks of wood to build a complex intersection of slopes and roads for his trucks and spent some time fitting it all together. He was later observed repeatedly wheeling a tyre through a puddle on the path and looking at the wet tracks left behind.

Another targeted trajectory is Dab. Sometimes our reflexes are just not fast enough to move away when a child is intent on poking, headbutting our chest or grabbing at our faces. Some children may hit, kick and knock down other children. Dynamically, the Dab schema relates to behaviours where children poke, point, jab, pinch and kick. Figuratively, dabs often represent things symbolically in the things that children draw or paint, such as eyes, flowers, buttons and fingers with tips. These indicate that children are developing an understanding of quantity.

Jack (2 years) was having a story read to him by his mum. He cuddled up next to her, pulled her arms toward him and began to pinch her arm, rolling the outer layers of her skin. Every time his mum moved her arm away, Jack began to cry and pulled it back. In his drawing Jack systematically made dots forming patterns. The series of dots represented a static image of the movement.

LJ (3 years, 4 months) was observed using a variety of marks in his drawing which included dabbing and horizontal and vertical marks. He said that the dabs were people in the park.

Emi Rose (2 years, 1 month) was observed at the easel, dabbing paint onto the paper. She later poked at a lump of dough.

Enclosure

The Enclosure schema is a bending of a trajectory. It is often seen in parallel with the Enveloping schema. Dynamically, children build enclosures with blocks, Lego, cushions and crates. Examples of related schemas include Infilling and Containment. Sometimes they build enclosures that they leave empty. Figuratively, children may use lines to enclose and surround their paintings and drawings. Sometimes children show an interest in edge ordering, which is where a child might make patterns on borders or place things on the edge of a border. Later, circles in drawings include heads, bodies, eyes, ears, hands, feet, animals, flowers, the sun or moon and wheels. Semi-circles are used to draw smiles, eyebrows, umbrellas and sometimes form parts of letters. Here, children are developing an understanding about being inside a boundary. Children will group and classify the things that they enclose, for example, a field of sheep, cows or horses. It is in this way that they learn to sort things into sets or groups and classify them.

Matt (2 years) was observed pushing and pulling a chair towards the kitchen sink. He climbed up onto the chair, then he stepped into the sink. He later climbed inside a box, pretending that it was a boat. He was later seen making a pattern with the blocks, the same enclosed structure over and over again.

Jo and Emma (both 4 years) decided to build a house from blocks in the corner of the room, which was already occupied by a small table and chair. Jo used this as the outline of the house and spent a long time building a boundary wall and a garden, while Emma made doorways and three separate bedrooms. Emma was later observed converting a large cardboard box into a doll's house.

Mustufa (2 years, 4 months) was observed playing with the train tracks. He joined the tracks together to form an enclosed track. He sat in the middle pushing the train around the track repeatedly. Later, he painted a picture which he enclosed with a border around the edge of the paper.

Infilling

This is when children fill in an enclosure in an ordered way. Children are learning about size and volume as they begin to estimate how many things they can fit into a space.

Issy (15 months) was observed taking objects out of a container and then putting them back in again.

Luke (2 years, 6 months) was observed filling cups with water, then pouring the water out. He then filled the cups with sand and tipped it out.

Jessy (3 years, 4 months) was seen to fill empty boxes with bits and pieces. She put some small pieces into the keyhole and was later seen putting the same size blocks into a box.

Containment

Children are exploring the idea of how they can fill things and, in this way, learning about volume and capacity – how much can they put into the container?

Jack (2 years, 2 months) was observed putting things into containers. He gathered a variety of small objects, such as farm animals, blocks and cars and put them all into a selection of containers.

Amy (3 years) was seen putting objects from all around the nursery room into a handbag. Later, she dumped blocks into containers to fill them.

Lilly (2 years) was observed throughout the day putting small items into a number of different boxes, trying to take things out of the boxes, and climbing into a box herself.

At home, she put objects into bags and filled buckets with water. During bath time she would fill one container from another. She played a game with her parents that involved guessing how many cups of water she would need to fill her bucket to the top.

Euclidian Enclosures

This schema also appears later and relates to how children co-ordinate trajectories. Dynamically, some children are interested in creating and exploring zigzags and angled enclosures. Figuratively, children may draw right angles, squares and triangles.

Pepe (4 years, 11 months) was observed building a complex enclosure with blocks, creating arches and ramps at each corner.

Twins Poppy and Annie (3 years) built a square enclosure in which they both pretended to be dogs. Later, they drew a number of pictures of dogs in cages.

Harry (4 years, 3 months) would frequently construct rectangular-shaped structures to park his cars in. He was observed drawing a detailed picture of the parked cars.

Enveloping

The Enveloping schema is often observed in parallel with Enclosure as a cluster – this means that children display more than one schema (Bruce, 1987). With the Enveloping schema, children are interested in completely covering objects and themselves. Dynamically, they will wrap things up, put things into bags or pockets, and enclose items in boxes and pots, covering them with lids. The child may wrap themselves in a blanket, get inside things and like to be cuddled. Figuratively, the child may paint over pictures and scribble over drawings. Children are learning about object permanence – how things can still exist even when they are out of sight. Children who wrap up and put a large collection of things into bags and drawers often display excellent memory skills if items are taken out, recalling what has been removed.

Carrie (3 years, 2 months) was observed playing with wet sand on a tray. She would repeatedly push all of the sand to one side into a mound and then push it back to cover the tray.

Emi (3 years, 8 months) drew a picture of a bird in a cage going to bed. She scribbled over her drawing and told her mum that the scribble was a blanket over the bird's cage.

Sophie (3 years, 11 months) was observed hiding things in a suitcase. She then wrapped up four blocks with newspaper and gave them to her friends as presents. She later did a painting and then covered up her picture with blue paint.

Inside/Outside is connected with Enveloping, where children place objects, and themselves, inside and outside of enclosures. Dynamically, children may climb in and out of a box or be interested in posting items in drawers. Figuratively, in their drawing they will place things inside and outside. For example, a child might draw a picture of themselves inside a house with rain outside.

Jo Jo (17 months) was observed getting inside a car where he pretended to be turning the steering wheel. Outside the car he locked the doors. He did this over and over again.

Anton (2 years) was feeling the inside of a selection of bowls – metal, woven and wooden. He was later seen climbing in and out of the laundry basket.

Josh (2 years) was seen to repeatedly climb in and out of a box.

Transporting

This is when children are absorbed with moving objects from one place to another. Dynamically, children may use a bag, pram or truck. Some children want to be transported in a pram, wheelbarrow or bike. Figuratively, transporting things from place to place helps children to understand changes in quantity. They learn about adding as they move one brick at a time. They also learn about taking away, space and direction as they move things from one place to another.

Nathan and Arty (3 years, 5 months and 3 years, 7 months) were observed stacking bricks in the wheelbarrow outside. They took turns to push it to the other end of the garden, unstacked the bricks, then restacked them. The boys did this over and over again.

Ross (18 months) moved his toy cars from one place to another, one at a time. He painted a picture which had lots of horizontal marks, representing his back and forth movements, which shows they have been internalised.

Elle (3 years, 2 months) was initially observed pushing a doll around in a pram. The pram was later transformed into a shopping trolley and she was seen taking things from around the room and putting them in it.

Connected with the Transporting schema is Heaping, where children bring things together, sometimes in random piles or in more structured arrangements. They will empty cupboards, leaving heaps of things all over the place.

Jules (19 months) was seen to collect boxes, cups, saucers, blankets, books, dressing up clothes and blocks. She put them all in a pile.

Robina (13 months) tipped her toys out of a container into a pile but was not interested in putting anything back in. She walked around the room gathering objects that she added to the heap.

Robyn (12 months) was seen outside tipping buckets of water and sand onto the ground. She filled a bucket with sticks, acorns, stones and leaves which she dumped by the door. She was later seen tipping the blocks out of the box.

Scattering is also part of the Transporting schema. This is where children may scatter objects by tipping them onto the floor. Dynamically, they may hand out objects to others or spread their objects everywhere.

Dilan (15 months) spent a considerable amount of time with the dustpan and brush trying to sweep up the sand that he had deliberately scattered on the floor. Each time he collected a large amount of sand he scattered it again. At home he enjoyed feeding the fish, throwing bread out for the pigeons, and planting seeds in the garden.

Nadia (2 years, 4 months) was seen at the table watching a group of children playing dominoes. When the game finished, she scattered the dominoes out of the box and walked away. She opened the cupboard and completely emptied it, scattering its contents.

Jay (15 months) moved from one thing to another, scattering everything around him on to the floor. He scattered all the toys in the baskets onto the carpet and wiped all of the toys off the table. He was seen using his legs to scatter the balls.

Rotation

This is where children are interested in and stimulated by things that rotate, twist and turn. Some children like to spin in circles until they are dizzy – others spin the wheels on toys again and again. Dynamically, children will explore taps, wheels, cogs, cylinders and other equipment. They may rotate their arms and bodies, walk and ride in circular movements, or pull toys round and round on a string. Figuratively, they will make circular scribbles and spirals and build structures with rotating parts. Children often use circles symbolically in their drawing to represent things. They understand how to rotate themselves and playthings.

Enda (4 years, 9 months) was sitting at the table with several other children. He rolled out a small piece of dough and using a small round cutter he placed pieces into a tray with six compartments. He then got a much bigger piece of dough and said he needed it so that he could stretch it to make more.

James (2 years, 4 months) was observed feeling the inside of a wooden bowl. Later, he was seen with a wooden spoon, swirling it round in circles.

Alysia (2 years, 9 months) was tracing her finger around the edge of a circular table. She went to the easel where she painted circular marks, then picked up a car, turned it upside down and rotated the wheels.

Connected with Rotation is Semi-Circularity, where children are interested in creating semi-circles. This schema allows children to practise the skills they need for writing letters of the alphabet. Dynamically, they run back and forth in a semi-circle or place items in a half-circle arrangement. Figuratively, some children may use semi-circles in their painting and drawing to graphically represent parts of the body, such as eyebrows, a smile, ears and closed eyes. They may also depict arches and rainbows.

Adelle (4 years) was observed trying to create an arch for the doorway of a house that she was constructing. Several days later she connected straws, making a structure that had up and down curves. It stretched across the construction area and connected to a chair.

Antonia and Joanna (4 years, 11 months and 4 years, 9 months) were constructing a railway track using only the curved pieces. Antonia later painted several pictures filled with semi-circles and then ran back and forth repeatedly in a semi-circle.

Sean (5 years) ran back and forth in a semi-circle and was observed tracing the edge of his cup in a semi-circle. He later created curved lines and was seen using curved blocks to create an enclosure.

Part of this schema is Core and Radial mark making, which may frequently appear in children's drawing and painting. Here they are interested in extending vertical and horizontal lines from a central core. Dynamically, it is seen in children's physical movements, where they have internalised and co-ordinated the Trajectory and Rotation schemas with vertical and horizontal movements. Figuratively, they understand how to use symbols to stand in for real things in the physical world. This is an important schema as children will need to understand how to use symbols in order for them to read and write. Some children create drawings of the sun with rays, wheels with spokes, flowers with petals, insects with legs and hands with fingers. To represent people, they draw a central core (circle) to represent the head and body, then add horizontal arms and vertical legs extending from the core.

Anna (3 years, 7 months) was initially observed making marks in the dry sand tray. She added water and made very different marks – the outline of a circle with a diagonal through it. She then collected some leaves and sticks from the garden and used these to represent a picture of 'her mum'.

Cassie (4 years) created a rotational structure using Lego, with several radials extending from it. She said that it was her 'umbrella'.

Sean (5 years, 9 months) used paper straws to make a helicopter rotor. He experimented with glue and tape as a means of fixing the base.

Connecting

Connecting is where children are interested in fastening and joining things together. They may connect train tracks or use string, wool, elastic bands and rope to tie things together or to themselves, sometimes in complex ways. An example of dynamic play would be using interlocking bricks, such as Stickle Bricks. Figuratively, drawings or paintings often have linked parts. With the Connecting schema, children are learning about fitting things together, such as train tracks or nuts and bolts, or fastening and connecting different materials using nails, tape, string or glue.

Paul (4 years, 8 months) was at the woodwork bench making a tree from balsa wood. Each time he attached a new branch to the tree it fell over. He explored how far a branch would extend in any direction before the tree tipped over.

Katie (3 years) was observed connecting magnetic trains together. She then went on to thread buttons and beads together and did a drawing showing connecting dots and lines.

Joy (3 years, 8 months) was observed making a necklace and bracelet with a one, two, three pattern using the red, yellow and green beads. She later ran string from one side of the role play area to the other.

Part of this schema is Disconnecting, where children are interested in separating things in reversible or irreversible ways. They may knock down towers built by others or take trains apart.

Nile (3 years, 1 month) disconnected 12 train carriages and then lined them up side by side.

Cammy (11 months) repeatedly knocked down sandcastles built by other children and then tried to separate a trailer from a truck.

Lucy (3 years, 5 months) was observed pulling a lump of clay into small pieces then pressing it back together again. She later pulled a leaf apart outside.

Positioning

Some children may place objects or themselves in a particular position – on top, underneath, in front, around the edge, behind, next to, up and down. Dynamically, children may line up cars and trucks, animals, teddies and dolls. Others may move cars and trains over and underneath bridges. Figuratively, children's drawings and paintings are frequently ordered with lines or dabs.

Perry (3 years, 7 months) lined up all of his cars in front of the kitchen door, saying that it was a traffic jam. He painted a picture of two long horizontal lines in front of a house, saying that it was the main road.

Haley (4 years, 4 months) positioned the farm animals so that the sheep were next to the lambs and the calves next to the cow. She was later seen turning and positioning the animals in a line.

Libby (4 years, 2 months) put a row of blue pegs in front of a green row, creating a repeating blue and green pattern. She later lined up the pencils, sorting them by colour.

Part of the Positioning schema relates to Ordering, where children are interested in arranging items by colour, shape, size, pattern and number. Dynamically, children may sort buttons according to size or colour. The sequence of things is important as well. Figuratively, children will systematically classify things by drawing them in order. They are learning how to arrange things in order of characteristics such as width, height and length.

Roberta (5 years) was observed playing with the farm animals. She arranged the animals in order of size from biggest to smallest. Later, she painted a number of pictures of her family, with her dad being the tallest and her baby brother the smallest.

Jani (4 years, 8 months) sorted and classified the blocks, putting them on the shelves according to their shape and size.

Daniel (3 years, 3 months) placed coloured pencils and crayons in a line, arranged from biggest to smallest. His drawings showed lots of ordered lines.

One to One Correspondence is the beginning of the development of an important mathematical concept. For example, a playing child may give a cup to each doll at a picnic. The child is matching, so that there is the same number of dolls to cups. This is an important schematic concept. Without an understanding of this concept, counting becomes meaningless.

Adam (4 years, 6 months) carefully drew around his fingers and thumbs. He was delighted to discover there were five each time he counted the digits.

Jennifer (5 years) was setting the table at home, singing as she did so, 'A plate for mummy, a plate for daddy, a plate for Vivian and a plate for me.'

Sarah (4 years, 1 month) was observed putting clay eggs that she had made into an egg box.

Topological

This is where children are interested in space and order, such as the straightness of lines and angles, either inside, outside, under, behind, on top or above, and next to. It includes understanding the order of points, betweenness and curves, which is dependent on understanding measurement. Sometimes Topological is referred to as the Orientation schema.

Jackson (4 years, 4 months) was observed making a complex bridge from blocks. He drove the cars over the bridge and the boats sailed underneath.

John (2 years, 3 months) was rolling balls inside a bowl. He turned the bowl upside down and placed the balls on top. He then placed a small whiteboard over the empty bowl, placed his hand underneath and said, 'The train goes under.' He placed the whiteboard vertically outside the bowl, dropped the balls behind, and said with a smile, 'Where they gone?' He spent some time experimenting with the whiteboard to find various places for it to pivot on the edge of the bowl. Later, he stuck a pencil through the top hole on a piece of file paper, noticed the angle of the paper and said he had made a 'crane'. He placed the bowl on his head saying it was a hat and an umbrella. He held the bowl in front of himself and said it was a 'steering wheel'. He rolled it on its edge (pretending it was a wheel). He put all the balls in the bowl, put two pens in the middle, said it was a 'birthday cake' and sang Happy Birthday to himself! (Adapted from Louis, 2022: 14).

Conrad (4 years, 9 months) was observed playing with the pulley, pulling up buckets of dry sand with a rope. He repeatedly pulled the rope up and down and seemed interested in the connections of the pulley itself. He added water to the sand and was heard to say, 'The bucket is much heavier to pull to the top.'

Orientation

Orientation is linked to Piaget's concept of space, and sensory and movement development. Children are interested in seeing things from a range of different viewpoints. Babies, toddlers, and young children will show a preference for how they want to be moved or held. Dynamically, they may hang upside down or go down the slide headfirst.

Figuratively, children may draw or paint a house in front of a tree or wall, or paint people and objects in front of or behind others.

Billi (9 months) was observed repeatedly climbing on the top of the table. She was later seen climbing on different size boxes. Outside she sat at the top of the slide.

Samuel (4 years, 3 months) was on a seesaw with his younger brother saying, 'I am up in the air and can see the top of the trees and you can only see the ground.' He drew himself high up, touching the trees, and his brother touching the ground.

Children also develop their spatial awareness by going through a boundary as opposed to under or around it.

Charlotte (2 years, 9 months) was pushing her frisbee through the metal railings repeatedly. She then rode her scooter through the puddle, making straight and curved tracks, before going through her mum's open legs.

Nathan (4 years, 11 months) was playing with the pegs and peg board. He used all the green pegs to fill in the rows from the top, then randomly used the remaining pegs for the rest of the rows. Several weeks later, Nathan filled in a peg board starting at the outside border.

Reflection

- Are there continuously available resources and natural materials for children to handle and transport freely?
- Are you involved, interested and observing schematic play?
- Are you knowledgeable and confident about the developing concept behind particular schemas?

Conclusion

It is vital that ECE students recognise what kind of learning is going on, identify what concepts children are trying to develop their understanding of, and support it.

References

Athey, C. (1990) *Extending Thought in Young Children: A Parent-Teacher Partnership.* London: Paul Chapman Publishing.

Bruce, T. (1987) *Early Childhood Education.* London: Hodder & Stoughton.

Louis, S. (2022) 'A Froebelian Approach. Observing Young Children'. London: Froebel Trust.

The Welsh Government (2021) *A Curriculum for Funded Non-Maintained Nursery Settings* (Consultation Document). Cardiff: The Welsh Government.

7
INTERPRETING LEARNING

Introduction

In this chapter, we will explore what interpreting children's learning from observations actually means in practice. Interpreting and assessment are interconnected and important parts of the observation cycle. How ECE students interpret young children's learning matters for three reasons. First, students must know what to look for and at when observing children's voices, actions and behaviours, and interpret what they are learning and thinking. Second, our interpretations affect how we get to know and understand a child and influence the appropriate support and opportunities that we offer them. Third, our interpretations act as a filter through which we teach, engage and interact with children.

It is vital that ECE students are aware of what they bring to the observation process. Although observations should be based on facts, our interpretations are not. Interpretations are not neutral or value free – they are influenced by our lived experiences, values, beliefs, culture and professional knowledge. These are important factors that we must be aware of when we observe children, as they have an impact on how we tune in and respond to them.

Lived Experiences

Our lived and personal experiences influence who we are as educators. Our families, parents, siblings, grandparents, friends, education, media – how we see people and things represented – all shape who we become. These experiences act as filters when we make judgements on the things we see children do.

For example, a four-year-old Black girl tells her teacher that she can't find any books featuring children that look like her. The teacher replies, 'Don't worry dear, have a look at this book', and hands the girl a book about a White child and a dog. The teacher is unconsciously telling her that she does not matter. If done frequently enough, this will have a negative impact on the girl's developing sense of identity. Disturbingly, by the end of the first term this little girl was drawing herself as a White child. Students need to recognise how this teacher's attitude has affected the child's sense of worth and how this might have an impact on their developing sense of identity and self-esteem. Would it matter more if it was a White girl? If so, why? All children need to see themselves represented, so that they can see people who look like them and their families. When educators discriminate against children, consciously or unconsciously, they not only cause them emotional and intellectual harm, but they may also prevent children from reaching their goals. This, in turn, stops them from accessing a rich and broad curriculum.

Beliefs

We all have our own beliefs about the children and families that we work with, even if we are unaware of them. Our beliefs and values influence our attitudes, expectations and assumptions about them. Our beliefs are reflected in both our observations and our interpretations because they directly affect how we see and provide support to children, how we interact and communicate with them, and whether we have low or high expectations of them. We all have a degree of bias and a tendency to feel more comfortable with things and people that are familiar. Our unconscious bias tends to develop with people and things that are unfamiliar (see Chapter 2 for different types of unconscious bias). Our observations and interpretations of children are based on our lived experiences and beliefs.

For example, if an educator believes that Black boys are overactive, noisy and rough, rather than providing them with an opportunity to be outside where they can develop physically, cognitively and socially, they may instead insist that the Black boys have to develop their concentration skills through indoor teacher-led activities. It is clear that labelling Black boys in this way will inevitably deny them access to a rich curriculum. Students should be aware that unconscious bias can lead to incorrect interpretations, resulting in not following children's interests or planning for them appropriately, thereby affecting their development, learning and progression. We cannot say with any certainty that we know how our beliefs about individuals or groups of children may affect our practice, unless we take time to reflect on those beliefs.

Professional Knowledge and Skills

The *Effective Provision of Pre-School Education* (EPPE) study (Sylva et al., 2004) identified two factors that affect the quality of pre-school provision. These are the levels of qualifications that staff have along with sensitive adults who interact with, respond to and engage with children. The Nutbrown Review (2012) reported that, to be effective, educators need to be skilled in making careful observations.

It is absolutely essential that ECE students who work with babies, toddlers and young children have an in-depth knowledge and understanding about how children develop and learn through play. If students do not know or understand how children develop and learn then they will be unable to adequately extend and support them. Students also need to understand the different purposes of observation techniques, as well as when and how they should use them (see Chapter 2 for ways of observation). Students should reflect on how their knowledge of child development and how their Observation, Assessment and Planning skills translate into their own practice.

For example, a student may observe that one of the children has difficulty joining in play during group activities. During the planning meeting, the student shares this observation with others and listens carefully to the different perspectives. The student will then use the information to provide support through modelling play for the child, as well as considering how best to support the child's independence.

Before a student can support and extend an individual child's learning, they must first learn how to make sense of their observations objectively. This process is called interpretation, analysing the observations that have been gathered over time. This involves thinking more deeply about the complex and connected ways that the child learns and reflecting on what they are capable of. Students need to think seriously about what the child's actions and behaviour might mean. Only then is it possible to plan a learning environment that is developmentally appropriate for the children attending. ECE student observations should capture what children can do independently – this then makes it easier to know what areas of development and learning that they are competent in. ECE students also need to consider how they are meeting children's learning and holistic development needs. It is essential that students are aware of the areas of development where children may require additional support.

Regardless of students' ethnicity, all ECE students should reflect on their conscious and unconscious biases and tendency to stereotype children and their families. Reflecting on your own personal bias can help you to take responsibility for your behaviours and make improvements to your professional practice. When students interpret their observations of children's learning, they will be drawing on their knowledge base and their own personal lived experiences. These will influence and shape their interpretations. This is why it is so important for observations to be presented as objectively as possible, based on what the observer sees or hears. This means that students should gather factual observations about children's development and learning, giving as much description as possible. If the information that students are gathering is based on their personal beliefs, then this is subjective and based on guesses rather than being factual (Louis and Betteridge, 2020). Observations are ultimately about capturing a child's actual development, interests, perspectives, feelings, ideas and interactions. One way of putting together all of the information gathered about a child's learning, interests and development is to think about the child from a colleague's perspective. When you share or discuss your observations with them, do they share the same opinion as you or are they offering an alternative perspective? What is most helpful here to the observer is being able to look at the child and their learning more deeply (Louis, 2020.)

The work of the following theorists is important in learning how to thoroughly observe the children that we work with, so that their play is effectively interpreted, and meaningful ways to support their development can be planned. It is recommended that students study Friedrich Froebel (1887) for his insight on play being superior to other forms of human development and his focus on the whole child, as well as his emphasis on the importance of observing children in the natural environment; Lev Vygotsky (1978), for the concept of the Zone of Proximal Development (ZPD); Susan Isaacs (1930), for her meticulous observations which allowed observers to step into the child's shoes; Jean Piaget (1969), and the techniques that he used with his own children; and Chris Athey (1990), who focused on cognition, schemas, what interests a child and what they freely choose to do. These theorists show us possibilities about detail that might be noticed in our observations, as well as the absence of behaviours that they thought of as significant.

Observations are also a means of communicating to the parent about the child's thinking and learning. Often, parents only have information about formal curriculum goals and think that is how practitioners judge learning. Sharing observations is a means of sharing professional knowledge in an accessible way to understand how practitioners define 'learning'. ECE students need to establish relationships with children and make connections between what is known and what is new to the child. An essential part of the ECE student's role is helping children to see the connections in their learning. Observing children systematically will help students to better understand the children and families that they work with, ensuring that they have meaningful learning experiences.

ECE students will be observing all of the time, sometimes almost subconsciously. How students interpret, use and share their observations is an important part of the process. Students will need to interpret the following developments:

- Physical – gross motor skills and fine motor movements and co-ordination, use of space.
- Intellectual – development of problem solving, imagination, creativity, concentration, memory.
- Language – speaking, listening, body language verbal and non-verbal, drawing, reading, writing, as well as drama, story-making, representation of own ideas and symbols, and social skills. Expression and communication of thoughts and ideas are also part of this.

- Emotional – control of emotions, showing of emotions, empathy, sympathy, happy, sad, angry. Making choices and decisions.
- Play – playing alone, alongside another in parallel play, associative, co-operative, symbolic, creative, imitation, playing games with rules.
- Behaviour – self-control and self-discipline, risk taking.
- Spiritual – children's sense of awe and wonder.
- Moral – understanding of rules and consideration for own behaviour, knowing right from wrong and taking responsibility for the consequences of their actions.
- Cultural – language, values, traditions and beliefs.

Interpretations

When ECE students observe, they capture the child in the moment, and they are more able to reflect on their observations if there are connections or patterns. Students should also consider what has been observed and decide on what that says about the child's strengths and interests. Interpretations are our own thoughts about what has been observed. This is how we make sense of observations – interpreting what the children have been observed doing and saying, while capturing their uniqueness.

Students may observe things about the child's development that concerns them. They may also want to think about how the child's behaviour is affecting their development or whether there is a cultural explanation to their explorations. It is important to keep in mind that children will develop their knowledge, skills and understanding in different ways. This is particularly important because it will provide additional information to help interpret and understand the child's actions and behaviours. All observations should aim to make the child's inner thinking visible.

Observation 1

Taylor (4 years, 3 months) and Arthur (4 years, 5 months) were discussing how to build a house for a toy bear, where to have the garage for his cars and where his room could be. They were working and negotiating together and trying to make sure that they would build a perfect house for the bear.

Interpretation

In this example, a good description of what the boys were doing has been given, but there is no sense of what they are thinking, exploring and learning, their unique way of playing, and how this affects what was observed. If we do not know what the child is thinking, how can we support or extend them adequately?

Observation 2

Katie and Ava (4 years) were cooking food for a 'baby' in the role-play area. Katie was talking to Ava saying, 'It is burning this pot.' Ava did not reply because she was busy stirring her own pot. Then Katie decided that hers was ready and she went to tell a practitioner that she had prepared food for the baby.

Interpretation

This shows Katie and Ava's experience and knowledge of preparing meals. Ava was involved in the process while Katie pretended that the food was ready to be eaten and this helped to develop her play into a story. This is a much better interpretation because it captures the voice and actions of the child. How we write up our observations can influence how we expect children to behave and how we interpret their actions, behaviours and words. Writing up brings another level of interpretation which students need to be aware of. Observations are the things that we see and our interpretations are what we think is happening in what we have seen. In that sense, observations – if written factually – are much easier to agree upon than interpretations.

For example:

Sara (3 years, 1 month) smiled after she made a necklace.
Sara was **happy** after she made the necklace.
Sara was **happy because she did not have to make another necklace**.
Sara smiled **cheekily** after she made the necklace.
The text in bold shows interpretations that are not based on fact.

When writing up observations, stick to the facts of what children are seen doing without judgement or assumptions – but, at the same time, it is necessary to capture the unique qualities of each child. This means capturing their voices and what they say, the way that they express their feelings and ideas, and how they describe, classify and categorise things.

It is vital that observations are a description of what is seen and heard, so that valid assessment judgements can be made based upon them. We can then focus our interpretations on how children learn, what they learn, and their interests. Writing up observations is helpful in ordering our thoughts and understanding the significance in what has been seen – but it takes time and practice. Interpreting observations of how children learn requires us to think more deeply about what the child is doing while drawing on our knowledge of them. This means thinking about how the child articulates their understanding through their play.

Observation 3

Nikki (2 years, 3 months) repeatedly scooped up handfuls of dry sand then watched it flow through her fingers. She moved sand from the tray onto the table, using only her hands. All the time she watched it flow through her fingers. She then patted the sand on the table down.

Interpretation

Nikki is working hard to make sense of the materials that she has encountered. She transforms the sand from something fluid and tries to make it ridged. She is using her senses to try to understand.

Interpreting children's interests requires students to focus their interpretations on the child's actions, behaviours and words, while reflecting on what might be behind them. In other words, what is motivating and engaging the child? Consider what interests the child and what they freely choose to do, their thinking, what the child talks about, their emotional response, and what they can manage physically.

Observation 4

Anna (3 years, 7 months) and Ella (3 years, 4 months) decided to tell stories to each other. Anna's story was about a little girl who had no mummy and she had to do everything, including taking the dog for a walk and listening to the sounds they heard along the way. She asked Ella questions about what was making the sounds. Ella recited the same story that a practitioner had read in its entirety, adapting it so that she was the main character.

Interpretation

Anna adapted the story *Bye Bye Baby* by Janet and Allan Ahlberg. I think that she was using her first-hand experiences of walking the dog in her story to help her make sense of the sounds that she heard and what the sounds belonged to. Ella repeated the story that was read and adapted it. She shows understanding of both the content and character. This is a story that she knows very well.

Interpreting what children have learned requires students to understand that children absorb knowledge through play and interaction as they engage with a range of experiences. Experiences may include everyday interactions with others and materials, talking and listening, observing, imitating and pretending, and learning through trial and error and experimentation. ECE students need to draw on their knowledge of child development to determine what children have learned.

Observation 5

Rosie (3 years, 3 months) was playing on her own with some stacking cups. She put the big cup into the little cup, but it did not fit. She tried putting the smaller cup into the bigger cup. After much problem solving and exploring different orders, Rosie figured out how to put the smaller cups into the larger ones.

Interpretation

This demonstrates how Rosie is able to concentrate in order to solve the problem at hand, whilst also learning about size.

After making our observations we can then respond appropriately, planning meaningful activities for the children that will interest and engage them. ECE students' interpretations of what they see are central to the Observation, Assessment and Planning cycle because this informs us of child development and what children need. This requires us to interpret children's development needs, voices and interests and reflect upon what they are doing and saying.

Susan Isaacs (1930) learned much about children from her close and attentive observations of them, which led to the development of a framework aimed at analysing and interpreting young children's self-initiated play and activity. Isaacs called this framework Discovery, Reasoning and Thought: Records. In it she identified four main categories – application of knowledge; increase of knowledge (problem and experiment, observation and discovery); social interchange of knowledge; and miscellaneous. Her framework can help students interpret and identify how children use their powers of reasoning, thinking and discovery in their play. The examples that follow illustrate the different types of knowledge under the headings that Isaacs identified.

Application of Knowledge

The application of knowledge relates to how children use it in its different forms in situations and problem solving. Isaacs breaks this down into sub-categories.

1. Formal and Theoretical Application

Sarah (3 years, 7 months) had recently been to a birthday party in a tower block. Later, she was looking at a book with pictures of high-rise buildings and said, 'When you are at the top everyone looks small and when you are on the ground floor everyone is the right size again.'

Interpretation

Sarah has brought together her sensual experience of seeing the pictures of buildings with the knowledge she has gained from her previous experience of being in a tall building. She knows that the height of the building affects how we see people's size. When ECE students are interpreting children's learning they need to be aware of how children are applying their existing knowledge. This links to Bruce's network for learning.

2. Imaginative and Hypothetical Application

Michael (4 years, 8 months) asked his father to take him to the park. His father said that he had to do the cooking. Michael said, 'What if we have a snack now and go to the park? You can cook when we get back.'

Interpretation

Michael is exploring the possibilities and consequences of different aspects of his situation. He shows that he is able to think imaginatively about an alternative reality. He is able to reflect on possibilities.

3. Make-Believe and Dramatised Knowledge

Josh (3 years, 11 months) played a game of the three little pigs with the farm animals. He pretended to be a policeman who had arrested the wolf for breaking into the house and put him in jail.

Interpretation

This example of make-believe play shows that Josh knows the story so well that he is able to dramatise it and make it his own. Again, we can make some useful links here with Bruce's 12 features of play, specifically pretend play.

4. Comparisons and Analogies

Nicky (4 years, 3 months) watched a group of children building and demolishing towers of blocks. He said, 'They look like people bulldozers.'

Interpretation

Nicky is comparing the function of the bulldozer with the children knocking down the blocks. He is observing how things can be the same but also different.

5. Practical Insight and Resources

According to Isaacs, children may also apply their knowledge in a practical rather than a theoretical or dramatised way.

Dylan and Theo's ball had gone over the fence and they could not reach it. Dylan was speaking to Theo about how they could get it back. Theo got a stick and tried to reach the ball but it was not long enough. Dylan stretched his arm under the fence with a ruler but he could not reach the ball. Both boys used sticks to try to bring the ball closer.

Interpretation

It did not take Theo long to figure out that his stick was not long enough. He poked a longer stick under the fence and moved the ball nearer. Both boys worked to find a solution to the problem at hand.

Increase of Knowledge: Problems and Experimentation, Observation and Discovery

Etienne saw a stick floating in the water tray and played with it for a while. He put pebbles and fir cones in the water to see if they would float or sink. Following his experiment, Etienne reported that 'all of the light things float'.

Interpretation

Etienne's comment signals that he has gained knowledge. This observation allows students to see how Etienne is constructing his knowledge through his experimentation.

Alex (4 years, 5 months) was watching Holli (4 years, 3 months) pour flour onto the weighing scales. She said, 'The scales go up and when this goes down, that goes up. It's just like a seesaw. I go up and you go down on the ground.' Holli replied, 'When I am down, you are up.'

Interpretation

In this example we see experimentation, observation and discovery as the girls encounter a new situation with the scales. They are both able to connect with their previous experience of being on the seesaw.

Social Interchanges of Knowledge

Milo (5 years, 8 months) was talking to his grandma. She said, 'Oh Milo, you have grown so much.' Milo said, 'I'm half of mummy.' Grandma said, 'Oh, I think you are even more than half her size.' Milo then went to measure himself against his mum. 'I'm up to here, grandma,' he said, raising his arm more than halfway. 'If I stand on the chair I am as tall as mummy.'

Interpretation

Milo is learning about the concept of height while he is talking about his family size, comparing the height of his mother to himself. He shows an understanding of halves.

Whys, Becauses, and Other Logical Questions and Reasoning

Freddie (3 years) asked his mum why he had to go to nursery. She told him, 'Because I have to go to work.' Again, he asked her why. She replied, 'So that I can earn some money.' He asked, 'Why?'

Interpretation

This line of questioning is important to help Freddie learn. He is curious and interested and repeatedly asking 'why questions' helps him to gather information about the things he is interested in.

A practitioner asked Nadine (4 years, 5 months) if she would help to water the plants. Nadine asked, 'Why?' The practitioner replied, 'Why do you think?' Nadine said, 'Because they would die if they did not get water. I would die too.'

Interpretation

This shows that Nadine has an understanding that she needs to care for living things. The practitioner is drawing Nadine in with her questioning.

Discussions: Corrections and Self-Corrections

Michael (4 years, 3 months) was at the water tray with a practitioner. He said, 'The boat floats but it won't if there is water in it.' The practitioner asked, 'Why will it not float if there is water in it?' Michael replied, 'Because the water is heavy.' The practitioner asked, 'What does the heavy water do to the boat?' Michael said, 'It makes it sink.'

Interpretation

Michael's play with the boat has helped him to understand that water will make the boat sink.

Oliver (4 years, 5 months) had a tall thin box stuck to a milk carton. He tried to balance it with the thin box as the base, but the model fell over. He turned it over to see if it would work. It was steady. He chose a much larger box and stuck his model on the top. He tried to make it stand and it did not fall over.

Interpretation

In this example it is possible to see Oliver's thinking in trying to figure out how to get his model to be stable. Oliver recognises the problem and is thinking about possible solutions.

Miscellaneous

The following observations, which do not fit into any of the groups, can be put under the heading miscellaneous.

Fraser (4 years, 3 months) said, 'I climbed so high I was nearly in heaven.'

Nerhia (4 years, 7 months) said, 'I had so much chicken wings yesterday that now I can fly high in the sky.'

This useful framework can help students to see the many different ways in which young children apply knowledge. While many of the observations overlap, the framework highlights children's thinking and learning. Students may use it to guide their interpretations of young children's interests, strengths and significant learning.

Interpreting Learning using Vygotsky's Zone of Proximal Development

Lev Vygotsky (1978) was interested in how adults and the environment affect and shape children's development and learning. Vygotsky (1978: 86) defined the Zone of Proximal Development (ZPD) as 'the distance between the actual development levels determined by independent problem solving, and the level of potential development, as determined through problem solving under adult guidance or in collaboration with more capable peers'. In other words, the ZPD is the development that a child can achieve independently and with guidance.

The role of the adult in interpreting children's learning is important here – students must understand children's actual development and have some knowledge of their individual characteristics. They must not only assess and interpret development but also be able to work with and alongside the child in order to support them to move into and through the ZPD. Vygotsky's ZPD is a useful guide for interpreting not just our interactions, but also how we support learning to advance children's development.

Observation 1

Helena (4 years, 3 months) was playing in the water tray, carefully filling several tall bottles. The student asked Helena if she could pour all the water in the bottle into a shorter jug. Helena looked at the tall bottle, then at the shorter jug, and said, 'Of course I can.' Helena poured the water into the jug. The student asked her if she had any water left in the bottle. Helena replied, 'Yes, lots.' 'Is the jug full?' the student asked. 'Yes,' replied Helena. The student then asked Helena to pour all the water into another short, but fatter, container. Helena emptied the bottle but the container was not full. Helena was puzzled because the bottle looked bigger than the container, but all the water fitted into it.

Interpreting this observation using the ZPD shows Helena's actual development – what she knows – that is, she is convinced that the taller bottle holds more water than the shorter jug. Helena's ZPD comes from the ECE student knowing that she finds it difficult on her own to understand that the quantity of water stays the same, even though it appears to change when poured into containers of a different size.

If ECE students work with children in their ZPD they are more likely to effectively interpret and facilitate children's learning and understanding.

Reflection

ECE students need to:

- Regularly interpret and reflect on their observations. This will help you to better plan for the next steps in learning.
- Use observations to facilitate and guide development and learning.
- Recognise that there are some skills that they will need to teach to children – but always start with what children already know and can do.
- Always observe children and respond to their interests.
- Recognise that interpretations will inform planning.

Conclusion

Interpreting observations can help students to better connect the description of what is happening for a child to what they think the child is doing. Taking time to reflect on what we think about children's developing learning is important if we are to support them effectively. The student's ability to interpret observations is essential to supporting the significant learning that has taken place for the child. Susan Isaacs provides us with a useful analytical framework to do this. Ultimately, students must get into the habit of questioning their interpretations in relation to what they think that children are doing, while unpicking the significant learning.

In the next chapter, we will explore the benefits of reflecting on observations and what students can do with the information they have gathered.

References

Athey, C. (1990) *Extending Thoughts in Young Children: A Parent-Teacher Partnership*. London: Sage.

Froebel, F. (1887) *The Education of Man*. New York: Appleton.

Isaacs, S. (1930) *Intellectual Growth in Young Children*. London: Routledge and Sons.

Louis, S. (2020) *How to Use Work Group Supervision to Improve Early Years Practice*. London: Routledge.

Louis, S. and Betteridge, H. (2020) *Unconscious Bias in the Observation, Assessment and Planning Process*. Foundation Stage Forum.

Piaget, J. (1962) *Play, Dreams and Imitation in Childhood*. New York: W.W. Norton.

Sylva, K., Melhuish, E., Sammons, P., Siraj-Blatchford, I. and Taggart, B. (2004) *The Effective Provision of Pre-School Education [EPPE] Project: Final Report*. London: Sure Start DfES Publications.

The Nutbrown Review (2012) *Foundations for Quality. The Independent Review of Early Education and Childcare Qualifications*. London: Department for Education.

Vygotsky, L.S. (1978) *Mind in Society: The Development of Higher Psychological Processes*. Cambridge, MA: Harvard University Press.

8

REFLECTING ON OBSERVATIONS AND LINKS TO THE CURRICULUM

Introduction

This chapter critically examines the process and impact of professional reflection, specifically that of reflective teaching. It considers the benefits of reflecting on observations of children and what ECE students do with the information they have gathered. This chapter will be aligned with planning and next steps in development and learning. It will also link observations to the relevant curriculum and focus on using observations to support, extend and improve learning. Discussions about planning feature throughout to prompt reflection. The importance of using observations to inform support and plan the learning environment is also discussed. This will help educators to put into practice the support necessary to extend children's experiences. It also discusses the importance of structuring the learning environment.

What is Reflective Practice?

Reflection is an active process of examining one's own observational practice and decision making in order to look at it in greater depth and learn from it. In this regard, reflection involves revisiting your observations, interactions and interpretations to gain a deeper meaning. When ECE students take time to think about what they have seen a child doing – whether it is a child taking responsibility or coping with change – it will lead to a greater insight into the child's holistic learning. Reflecting on practice in this way helps students to make effective decisions about how they plan to support or extend learning. In many respects, the reflection process challenges ECE students to be honest about their interactions and responses, what they have seen and heard, what they have recorded and what they think.

Pollard et al. (2008: 14) attempt to combine the method and process of reflection by drawing together seven characteristics of reflective teaching, saying, 'Reflective teaching implies an active concern with aims and consequences, as well as means and technical efficiency.' Their first characteristic draws attention to particular qualities of reflective teaching and learning, why these qualities are relevant and why they should form the foundation of reflective teaching. However, the language used is not expressive or precise enough and open to individual interpretations.

Dymoke and Harrison (2008) suggest that reflective teaching is more than a technical process – reflective understanding does not just happen overnight and is not solely based on 'technical efficiency' as proposed by Pollard et al. (2008). Reflection is seen as a progressive understanding that will represent effective teaching and learning later in professional practice.

Dymoke and Harrison explore the social, individual and political context of reflective teaching, suggesting that it requires a knowledgeable reflective individual.

> It is in its relationship with professional knowledge and practice that deeper reflection becomes such an important feature of the reflective practice. If reflective practice stays at a technical level, restricted to the evaluation of teaching and learning strategies and classroom resources, it would be difficult to stress its importance in teacher development. However, as reflective practice is used to explore more *critically* the underlying *assumptions* of learning and teaching, it adds to our professional knowledge. (2008: 9)

This is unlike what has been proposed by Pollard et al. (2008) in the first characteristics of reflective practice, where there is an underlying assumption that teachers will know how to critically reflect upon their own experiences. Pollard et al.'s model does not offer ECE students the scope for deep level reflection in the same way that Dymoke and Harrison (2008) do. The problem that confronts us has to do with the assumed willingness of ECE students to reflect on behaviour that they are not yet aware of themselves.

The second characteristic of Pollard et al. (2008: 14) illuminates the process technically: 'Reflective teaching is applied in a cyclical or spiralling process, in which teachers monitor, evaluate and revise their own practice continuously.' Whilst correct, this definition of the process is premature as it is the levels of deep reflection and self-examination that constitute meaningful reflection in action. Schon (1983: 69) says reflection in action is a rigorous professional process involving acknowledgement of and reflection on uncertainty and complexity in one's practice leading to a 'legitimate form of professional knowledge'. Quality of reflection is significant and important for ECE students because it will have a direct impact on the quality of teaching and learning, leading to much deeper levels of reflection and enhancement of practice.

Bolton (2005: 33) proposes, 'All aspects of ourselves are interrelated; practice is not undertaken with one part, and personal life another. They might be linked in surprising ways, moreover, by irrelevant-seeming factors. The insignificant-seeming incident, appearing seemingly out of nowhere in reflective practice writing, may be central.' According to Bolton (2005), it is not possible to separate our personal values and beliefs from our professional practice and identity. Reflection and reflexivity allow for critical links to be made between our actions, beliefs, feelings and values through our deep questioning about our practice and actions.

On the other hand, Bold (2008: 14) suggests that reflection can be conceptualised as 'unpeeling the layers of the onion'. She says that 'the outer layer' is a symbol of one's values and beliefs – for students the significance of values is inseparable from all aspects of reflection and reflectivity as it permeates throughout the onion so that every layer of it is affected.

Pollard et al. (2008: 26) take a middle position, as they suggest that, 'The aim of reflective practice is thus to support a shift from routine actions rooted in common-sense thinking to reflective action stemming from professional thinking.' Pollard et al. (2008) talk about routine actions and bad habits, suggesting that practitioners and students need time to think about their bad habits, reflect upon and do something about them, and in this way move reflection on to action or change. Pollard et al. (2008) imply that practitioners and students become tuned in and aware of their tacit behaviour through this 'spiralling process'. This suggests that there is a willingness on the part of the practitioner or student to break the circle of self-perpetuation and repetition. Pollard et al. (2008) are very technical in their approach to reflection – for them the interplay is between common-sense thinking and reflective action that is well established from professional thinking. Drawing on professional knowledge, Pollard et al. (2008) focus mainly on the technical methods used in reflective teaching and this is significantly different from what Bold (2008) and Bolton (2005) think are critical to its theory and practice. The relevance of other kinds of knowledge is a key factor when ECE students are faced with situations that are potentially problematic. Bolton (2005) brings this aspect to the surface and exposes the implicit and explicit values that underpin professional practice, saying that application and understanding are components which naturally go together when using reflection as a tool for improvement of moral and professional practice.

Pollard et al.'s (2008: 14) third characteristic suggests that reflection is an ongoing and continuous journey – 'Reflective teaching requires competence in methods of evidence-based classroom enquiry, to support the progressive development of higher standards of teaching.' Pollard et al. (2008) yet again assume a willingness by practitioners and ECE students to develop competence, thus widening the pool of practitioner and student knowledge that, in turn, enhances their practice. Pollard et al. (2008) draw attention to the method whereby appropriate application of methodology is seen as a necessary condition for higher levels of reflection and transformation of practice. The underlying assumption here is that practitioners and students will know about methodology and apply logic rather than emotions to their critical reflections. However, Boud et al. (1985: 194) argue that 'it is common for reflection to be treated as if it were an intellectual exercise, a simple matter of thinking rigorously. However, reflection is not solely a cognitive process, emotions are central to all learning.'

Similarly, Freire (2005: 15) proposes that 'authentic reflection cannot exist apart from action'. Action is a vital ingredient in and on the reflective process because when action is excluded from the process, our perceptions can become contaminated by our personal prejudices. Fook and Gardiner (2007) argue that reflection is much deeper than just thinking, as Pollard et al. imply. It is both theory and practice based on individual understandings and inseparable from the social world, a view which is similar to that of Dymoke and Harrison (2008).

Pollard et al.'s (2008: 14) fourth characteristic suggests: 'Reflective teaching requires attitudes of open-mindedness, responsibility and wholeheartedness.' However, this raises implications for personal–professional practice as key variables have been omitted. Pollard et al. (2008) draw on professional knowledge as the main route to challenge practice, proposing that practitioners have a personal commitment to question their language, behaviour and assumptions. Furthermore, if practitioners and students use reflective teaching to inform ongoing practice, the assumption is that they will ask questions that prompt reflection about what has happened, why, and what the impact has been. Real situations require practitioners and students to have real knowledge; knowledge comes from experience, both personal and professional. In the reflective teaching process, they have a dual importance within a social, personal and political context. Reflection is not about reaching a ceiling or crossing a line, it is about how ECE students see themselves as teachers and learners, able to draw on both personal and professional knowledge whilst being tuned into their underlying emotions, values and beliefs.

Boud et al. (1985: 19) put forward the idea that, 'Reflection is an important human activity in which people recapture their experiences, think about it, mull it over and evaluate it. It is this working with experience that is important to learning.' For ECE students, the interconnections between the values and morals that we use to guide us in how we make sense of or apply common-sense thinking to our experiences and our professional practice are not embedded in Pollard et al.'s (2008) conceptualisation of reflective theory.

Pollard et al.'s (2008: 14) fifth characteristic puts forward the notion that, 'Reflective teaching is based on teacher judgements, informed by evidence-based enquiry, and insights from other research.' Goodson (2003) argues that reflective practice is more than just reflecting on personal experience and that there is a need to have an awareness of the social and political context. Similarly, Bolton (2005: 5) suggests that practitioners' rights to make moral and professional judgements is being eroded – 'They are being reduced to technicians, their skills to mere technical competences. In order to retain political and social awareness and activity, professional development work needs to be rooted in the public and political as well as the private and the personal.'

It is in this way, according to Bolton (2005), that practitioners begin the process of reflecting on their morals and values, and personal and professional judgements. The problem unfolding with Pollard et al.'s (2008) theoretical conceptualisation of what reflective teaching should be is that it does not delve deep enough into the capacity of practitioners and students to uncover experiences whereby there is a sustained process of critical evaluation and awareness of developing pedagogy. Goodson (2003: 1) illuminates the interconnections that exists between reflection, knowledge and practice in teaching and learning and puts forward the idea, 'The forms of knowledge that we produce are often closely related to perceptions that we have of ourselves and the projections of ourselves that we undertake'. Much of ECE students' work will be based on assessment of others; therefore, the epistemology of knowledge through experience, and the processes and development of reflective practice, must not be underestimated. According to Schon (1983), this forms the roots to understanding who we are in the world, thus informing our professional judgements. Schon (1983) argues that it is possible to identify 'reflection in action' in which changes are made through reflecting on experience. Schon says:

> When someone reflects in action, he (sic) becomes a researcher in the practice context. He is not dependent on the categories of established theory and technique but constructs a new theory of the unique case. He does not keep means and end separate but defines them interactively as he frames a problematic situation. He does not separate thinking from action... His experimenting is a kind of action, implementation is built into his enquiry. (1983: 68)

Pollard et al.'s (2008: 15) sixth characteristic sharpens the focus – 'Reflective teaching, professional learning and personal fulfilment are enhanced through collaboration and dialogue with colleagues.' This theory is indeed persuasive as they put forward the notion that the exchange of ideas is central to building up knowledge.

Similarly, Bolton proposes that reflection is a crucial part of professional learning and development.

> Reflective practice is a process of learning and developing through examining our own practice, opening our practice to scrutiny by others, and studying texts from the wider sphere. Reflexivity is finding strategies for looking at our own thought processes, values, prejudices and habitual actions, as if we were onlookers. It is a focusing closer and closer. (2005: 7)

Pollard et al.'s (2008: 15) seventh and final characteristic proposes that, 'Reflective teaching enables teachers to creatively mediate externally developed frameworks for teaching and learning.' This paints a picture of a continuous cycle of reflection, whereby reflection is seen as a routine aspect of teaching.

The reflective practice model proposed by Pollard et al. (2008) was appropriate for its day. It presents a summary of theoretical analysis of the concept of reflection, thus opening the door for professional reflection. However, it plays down the centrality of the interconnections between personal and professional knowledge and the social and political – by doing so it does not allow ECE students to enter the room. This could be because not enough focus is placed upon practice and the individual's ability to critically examine their own personal, professional and pedagogical values and practice. However, Dymoke and Harrison (2008) take ECE students beyond the door and into the room by joining together reflective practice and professional knowledge. The purpose of reflection here is to delve deeper into your observations, routine actions and behaviours. The model proposed by Dymoke and Harrison (2008) is better equipped to help ECE students be both critical and reflective and deal with any underlying assumptions.

Reflecting on Observations

Every day, ECE students will be expected to observe, assess and plan and capture and support significant moments of development and learning. Reflecting on the observation process is important since it will help to ensure that students plan developmentally appropriate next steps in learning for children that seek to build on what they know and can do already. This means that ECE students will need to think carefully about individual children and what motivates them. How do they think and learn? Reflecting on the interpretation of observations that you and your colleagues have gathered of children systematically and over time will help you to plan more effectively for their next steps in development and learning.

Essentially, part of becoming a skilled observer requires ECE students to reflect on the objectivity of their observations, interactions and interpretations. It is also important that ECE students reflect on their knowledge and understanding of child development. As students observe babies and young children, they are learning about all that they can do. Students can then decide how to support or extend learning. ECE students have a valuable role to play in how they structure and organise the learning environment both inside and outside. Observations give students information about what sort of learning experiences they will need to provide children with, as well as revealing insights into what concepts children might be exploring. Reflecting on your observations is an integral part of the Observation, Assessment and Planning process.

Reflecting on Planning

By reflecting on their own observations, ECE students can develop their practice and a deeper understanding of their own knowledge. Reflecting helps ECE students to think more critically about their observations, interactions and interpretations as part of the Observation, Assessment and Planning process. It means looking at what you have recorded, what you think of it and why, and thinking about the process of the child's play. The more students reflect on their observations, the better they understand them.

Planning and the Curriculum

There are a number of different early learning curriculums being used in the United Kingdom. These include *Aistear*, the curriculum framework for children from birth to six years in Ireland; the *Curriculum for Excellence* for children from birth to 18 in Scotland; the *Early Years Foundation Stage* and *Birth to Five Matters*, for children from birth to five years in England; the new *Foundation Phase Curriculum* for children aged three to seven years in Wales; as well as the Froebelian approach, Rudolf Steiner curriculum, Maria Montessori curriculum and Reggio Emilia approach. Whichever curriculum framework students use, they should know how to navigate their way around it in order to provide children with developmentally well planned, challenging, motivating and meaningful learning experiences. They all require ECE students to plan meaningful activities in response to their observations in order to support children's development and learning.

ECE students who observe children objectively over a range of activities will discover for themselves what the child knows and can do. This knowledge about individuals or groups of children can help ECE students to develop the curriculum content in a way that supports the child's learning and development. When ECE students regularly observe, they are in a good position to begin to track children's interests and help with planning for them. Observations will give students insight into what motivates and intrigues children. Once they have recognised children's interests, the *Early Years Foundation Stage* (2012: 7) urges ECE students to 'plan first-hand experiences and challenges appropriate to the development of the children... Plan linked experiences that follow the ideas children are really thinking about'. When students pay close attention to all that babies and children are doing and saying they gain useful insight into their unique development.

ECE students may draw on different ways to record their observations. However, they will need to be tracked in order to check on children's progress. Students should always include the date on their observations, even if writing on Post-it notes. This information is vital in interpreting and understanding children's progression. It is also good practice to reflect on your interpretations of your ongoing observations.

ECE students will need to review everything that they have observed and also consider information that they have gathered from others about the child. For example, after observing Anna (5 years, 1 month) over several weeks, the student made the following notes:

- Anna has good physical coordination, can run, climb, pedal, jump and throw
- She is intrinsically motivated – participates in looking for worms and insects, took the magnifying glass to look more closely
- Shows interest in the labels for insects
- Sometimes gets frustrated and pushes other children away
- She is interested in blocks
- Participates in pretend play

How can ECE students use this information about Anna in planning the learning environment? Is Anna having a hard time expressing herself? How would you plan to support her? What sort of experiences could you plan to help her to develop self-control?

Children learn in a holistic way and it is vital that ECE students plan for children to have access to all areas of the curriculum. Observations will give students insight into what and how a child is learning and this information can feed into the planning process. The curriculums that ECE students use tend to have different ways of recording children's progress. ECE students need to make themselves familiar with whichever curriculum they use, so that they can better understand the assessment process and outcomes for children.

Resourcing the Learning Environment – Taking a Universal Mathematical Approach

It is essential to include play materials that children have at home, for example, cooking pots in three different sizes. This is echoed by *Aistear* (2009: 57) – 'A range of mathematical tools are provided, for example calculators, measuring tapes, rulers, height charts, weighing scales and phones.'

Opportunities for mathematical experiences and discussions are everywhere. Children show awareness of and are responsive to numbers and counting, which are used as they set the table at mealtimes. Numbers are part of everyday life – on hand and finger rhymes, legs on animals, two wheels on a bicycle, four wheels on cars, numbers on buses. Equally, children are sorting, classifying, making comparisons and solving problems all the time. Is it red? Is it ripe? Opposites and comparisons can look at bigger than, smaller than; wooden block play in making a bridge; a child putting two shoes on the right feet; doing up buttons and putting on coats. Children naturally explore shapes, space and measurement. In their everyday life experience, they come across things that are longer than, taller than or heavier than. Shapes are everywhere. Many fruits have a sphere shape.

Triangles and prisms are integral to strong buildings, goal posts and pitched roofs. Eating a slice of pizza helps children to learn about lines and point. Paper folding activities help children to move from flat to 3D. Children construct and build 2D flat designs using materials such as tessellations which require them to repeat patterns with a single shape, stick laying, or constructing railway lines and tracks. Children may also explore flexible lines and wavy lines with ribbons and streamers. Mathematical language can be found in many nursery rhymes and songs. In practical mathematics, children jump off things, they climb on, near and far. There is exploring topological spaces – over, under and through. *Realising the Ambition* (2020: 69) 'acknowledges your responsibility for your own professional learning around specific subject areas such as literacy and numeracy and mathematical development'.

Developmentally Appropriate Planning

Observation is key, as is knowing typical developmental sequences, so that differences with implications are picked up and acted upon. Louis provides a useful example:

> An educator was asked by the mother of Khadiya (7 months) to observe her at home. The educator noticed that Khadiya took items from people and picked up objects with her right hand. Her left hand appeared to be much weaker and she rarely used it to explore. Khadiya also crawled in an unusual roly-poly way and the educator had only observed two other children who crawled in the same manner. (2022: 20)

Khadiya was soon identified as having cerebral palsy and given excellent specialist help. What matters here is observation and knowledge and not age. Before ECE students can plan for children, they must interpret and understand their observations. This requires reflection. When interpretations are translated into planning, it should aim at making the child's inner thinking visible. If students do not know how the child is thinking and learning, how can they support or extend learning adequately?

An important part of the planning process is being able to offer children experiences that will both inspire and motivate them. Students will also need to consider how best to introduce new experiences to children that build on what they already know, incorporating meaningful opportunities for children to discover, investigate, engage and talk to others and ask questions. Make time to reflect on the next steps in planning which have been identified for individuals and groups of children.

Planning developmentally appropriate activities for individuals or groups of children requires ECE students to gather all the information that is known about the child. The people that you work with and the child's parents will all have pieces of information that you will need to bring together so that you have a picture of the child in context. It is only when all the pieces come together that ECE students can begin to plan. It is vital that

ECE students reflect on their observations as this process leads to offering children individual and meaningful learning experiences. Instead of using a one-off example, students will benefit from gathering observations across several weeks. Reflecting on three or four observations will support students' planning to help children to develop possibilities in that moment and beyond.

Observation

2nd August 2021

Mia (3 years, 3 months) found a Playmobil oil drum (about the size of an old-fashioned film canister). She gestured to the adult to fill it with water from the tap, then took the container outside to the fire engine at the far end of the garden. Going outside while holding the container filled with water seemed to be an important part of her play. She did this several times before deciding that it was time to drink the water.

10th August 2021

This is Mia today pulling the trolley in the sand.

16th August 2021

After watching her dad play cricket, Mia drew some cricket stumps on the sand so that she could play cricket with John.

24th August 2021

Walking along the street, Mia commented on each gate as to whether it was 'tossed' (closed) or 'hopem' (open) – initiated by herself.

What is Mia doing and what skills has she mastered? What little glimpses are there into how she is making sense of the world? How would you plan for Mia's Transporting schema which is developing alongside her Trajectory schema (lining things up)? What does her language development tell you? Is it on track? Look for patterns and connections in her play – how might you plan meaningful experiences with borders and perimeters to support interest in where the containing fence is, where the gate is and how to get out, and build on what she already knows?

Responsive Planning to Support Other Areas of Development

After spending some time studying the curriculum and reflecting on her observations of Joanna (3 years, 5 months), the ECE student realised that, although Joanna was very keen to write and hang around with the adults, she had no observations of Joanna socially interacting with other children. As a result, the student immediately focused on supporting the development of Joanna's relationship with her peers. The *Aistear* (2009) curriculum framework reminds us that 'many interactions just happen while others come about through careful planning and decision making'. Reflecting on observations allows the student to understand what milestones and development Joanna has achieved, as well as recognising other areas of development where she will need to plan meaningful learning experiences to capture any significant moments of Joanna's social interaction with her peers.

Structuring and Organising the Learning Environment

Once students have interpreted their observations in line with the specific curriculum framework that they are using, they will have a good idea about what children know and have developed and learned. By linking their observations with the curriculum, students will know what developmental milestones their children have reached. This important act requires students to draw on knowledge and understanding about the child and to plan for them based on the child's individual need.

Although ECE students are not responsible for formal structuring of the learning environment, it is certainly important, since this is a space in which children explore, create, think, imagine and develop with the support of observant, responsive and knowledgeable adults. ECE students are, however, responsible for the informal structure, as this is at the heart of what they do. Informal structure lies in the relationship that ECE students have with children (things like the boundaries, expectations and ethos that students create with children, parents and staff). Leadership is fundamental to structuring the ethos in which ECE students work and come together as a community.

Another vital informal structure is the physical environment, such as the garden and indoor areas – how students lay things out, what they provide, when children can access things, and how students encourage them to use what is there. The Reggio Emilia approach calls this the third teacher. Students need to think carefully and deeply about these things. In doing so they are informally structuring. How ECE students respond to and interact with children informally affects how they plan. Students will need to think carefully about how they structure the physical and emotional learning environments in response to children's interests.

Reflection

- How are your observations helping you plan for individual children?
- How are you making the child's thinking visible to all?
- How are you planning for children's individual and diverse needs?
- How engaged are you in examining and reflecting on your practice?

Conclusion

Reflecting on your observations will help you to gain vital insight into how best to support children's development and learning. Reflecting on your observations with colleagues gives insight into a number of different perspectives about your observational practice – feedback, suggestions and ideas can help students to improve their practice. An underpinning principle of all the curriculum frameworks used in the United Kingdom is that it is relationships with knowledgeable and reflective adults that give children autonomy, so that they can apply what they know and can do, helped by the adult when they cannot manage something. Knowing how to find the right help at the right time in the right way matters.

References

Bold, C. (2008) 'Peer support groups: Fostering a deeper approach to learning through critical reflection on practice'. *Reflective Practice,* 9(3): 257–67.

Bolton, C. (2005) *Reflective Practice* (2nd edn). London: Sage.

Boud, D., Keogh, R. and Walker, D. (eds) (1985) *Reflection: Turning Experience into Learning.* London: Kogan Press.

Dymoke, S. and Harrison, J. (eds) (2008) *Reflective Teaching and Learning.* London: Sage.

Early Education (2012) *Development Matters in the Early Years Foundation Stage (EYFS).* St Albans: Early Education.

Fook, J. and Gardner, F. (2007) *Practising Critical Reflection: A Resource Handbook.* Maidenhead: Open University Press.

Freire, P. (2005) *Pedagogy of the Oppressed.* New York: Continuum.

Goodson, I.F. (2003) *Professional Knowledge, Professional Lives: Studies in Educational Change.* Maidenhead: Open University Press.

Louis, S. (2022) *'A Froebelian Approach. Observing Young Children'.* London: The Froebel Trust.

National Council for Curriculum and Assessment (NCCA) (2009) *Aistear: The Early Childhood Curriculum Framework.* Dublin: National Council for Curriculum and Assessment.

Pollard, A., Anderson, J., Maddock, M., Swaffield, S., Warin, J. and Warwick, P. (2008) *Reflective Teaching: Evidence-informed Professional Practice* (3rd edn). London: Continuum International Publishing Group.

Schon, D.A. (1983) *The Reflective Practitioner: How Professionals Think in Action.* New York: Basic Books.

The Scottish Government (2020) *Realising the Ambition: National Practice Guidance for Early Years in Scotland.* Edinburgh: The Scottish Government.

9

OBSERVATIONS AS A TOOL – SHARING OBSERVATIONS WITH PARENTS AND COLLEAGUES

Introduction

This chapter considers observations in practice as a tool to facilitate learning. It explores the state of parental partnerships in practice and examines the challenges. The links between parents' personal knowledge and different ways of engagement are explored, along with practitioner knowledge. The frequency of reporting to parents is also covered. This chapter will also look at how to effectively share observations about children's learning and development in staff teams and with parents and children.

Although most of the observations presented throughout this book show the child as a scientist embarking on new and exciting learning, parents and carers will also have many similar everyday informal observations of their child behaving in different ways. In order to work with parents in meaningful ways it is vital that ECE students understand the distinction between play and learning. Play is not the same as learning, but play facilitates learning. According to Vygotsky,

> In play a child always behaves beyond his average age, above his daily behaviour; in play it is as though he were a head taller than himself. As in the focus of a magnifying glass, play contains all development tendencies in a condensed form and is itself a major source of development. (1978: 102)

In other words, it is a child's development that will determine a child's learning, but play is a leading factor in the child's development.

Parents' observations of their children at play can provide students with additional information about their development. Parents are in an ideal position to gather observations of their children's development, progress and learning. Parents will often observe their children modifying their ideas in their play. They will notice them refining and combining and remembering and developing their expectations. Indeed, parents support their children's learning in all aspects of their lives in order for them to do well at school and in life. There will be many activities that parents already do with their children at home. Sometimes ECE students just need to highlight the educational worthiness of the activity in order to facilitate learning – for example, encouraging parents to use resources and materials that best support children's progression, promoting the use of developmentally appropriate materials that children can explore independently, and providing children with open-ended materials so that they can both experiment and discover things for themselves. In practice, ECE students may be expected to model how to be supportive to children during play for parents and carers while being mindful not to be domineering. Students may also need to talk to parents about the things that they have observed or noticed about their child, encouraging them to share their observations of play episodes that children lead for themselves, or that are based on the child's interest.

When students share information with parents they can provide a greater insight into the processes of learning and why it is important. Using observations as a tool facilitates learning and creates opportunities for students to get to know every child. The process of sharing and receiving information from observations about specific children enables ECE students to respond and interact more appropriately with that child. Ultimately, the role of the student is to enable and respond to parents in facilitating their children's self-chosen play and explorations at home by demonstrating to the parent how their child is constructing knowledge and understanding. The experience of sharing information in this way can lead to ECE students changing the way in which they respond or interact with children.

Facilitating Learning

Good parental engagement is about understanding what is offered, seeing how their children engage with play and learning indoors and outdoors, having frequent opportunities to share information from home and school or the setting, and being engaged in as many ways as possible. These start with sound induction processes built through informal communication such as rolling images on the whiteboard, newsletters and practical workshops explaining how children play, develop and learn. These can be linked to the setting's ethos and why their child's development is unique. When parents experience quality time with their child's key worker, that is the time to involve them more, giving them simple things to do with the child or more specific tasks. Some schools and settings send slips home with children as prompts for parents to talk about achievements that happened during the day. This can be an important link for working parents between home, school and/or setting.

It is acknowledged that, in practice, it can be difficult for practitioners to find time to build genuine relationships with parents or carers. Melhuish (2007: 3) suggests that the key to successful working partnerships is to ensure that the intervention is designed to meet the needs of the child, parent and setting.

Early Years educators should:

- involve parents as well as children;
- provide intensive support to vulnerable parents in the first three years to enable them to meet their children's needs;
- avoid labelling 'problem families';
- target multiple risk factors;
- plan interventions that last long enough to make a difference and consult and develop these with parents;
- be culturally appropriate.

Sharing Observations with Parents

ECE students should respect and draw on the personal knowledge of parents and carers about their child. This recognises that parents have a powerful influence on home learning and it will help students to understand the influences on the child's life. This is echoed by the Qualification Curriculum Authority in England, cited in MacLeod-Brudenell (2004: 412): 'Parents are children's first and most enduring educators. When parents and practitioners work together in Early Years settings, the results have a positive impact on the child's development and learning. Therefore, each setting should seek to develop an effective partnership with parents.'

Similarly, research for the Effective Provision of Pre-School Education project indicates that parental partnerships are crucial for children's emotional wellbeing and development and learning. Parents are by far the most important and influential people in their children's lives. It is important for ECE students and practitioners to remember that children learn from their parents. According to Miller, Cable and Devereux:

Parents and families teach by example and through their attitudes: how to express emotion; how to respond to other people; how to behave 'appropriately' as a boy or a girl; how to love and care for others; and how to make sense of the world. A family's values, beliefs, fears and prejudices will, at least initially, be passed on to children. (2004: 39)

ECE students need to be able to inform parents and carers of the objectives and content of the curriculum framework and share knowledge of how their child is developing and learning. Wheeler and Connor state:

> The importance of working more effectively with parents to involve them in learning cannot be overstated. Children learn from everything they experience wherever they are and whoever they are with. The greater the continuity between home and setting and the richer the learning environment in both, the more the children will benefit. (2009: 130)

Challenges of Sharing Observations with Parents

We know that children are interesting and deep thinkers – they work very hard to make sense of the world around them and they each have their own unique way of doing this. It is the job of the ECE student to try to understand what and how they are learning so that they can match provision to them. However, not all parents will believe or acknowledge this. Some may tend to believe very much in the 3Rs and will have very formal views on education. Students have an important role to play in sharing their observations with parents so that they can explain the significance of the child's action and behaviours and the many steps taken in what the child is doing. This can reassure parents that every one of these prior steps experienced is valuable in its own right and should not be rushed. Parents may then come back with observations of their own to share.

Another challenge that ECE students may face is that, if they want to show parents something that their child has done, many parents will assume that the student is going to be talking about their child's bad behaviour. Such are the fearful relationships between parents and the setting. The parents feel that they have to be guarantors for their child's good behaviour and nothing else. Siraj-Blatchford, Clarke and Needham (2007: 53) draw on the work of MacNaughton to show how many parents conform: 'MacNaughton (2003) describes a "conforming process" that results in home-school contracts being created, in which parents had to conform to demands education made on them.'

The ethos in schools and settings of making and sharing observations with parents starts at the very beginning of a child going to nursery, often with a home visit, so it is explained and accepted as the foundation stone of good Early Years practice. Of course, parents also talk to each other about their observations and are reassured. Many parents enjoy seeing their children's learning journeys and the observations shown in it. This is a new thing for most parents but they look forward to those times with a key worker when they can discuss their child. However, in many schools and settings across the United

Kingdom in recent years, the number of children perceived to have developmental delay has increased, although there are many complex reasons for this. Sometimes parents find it difficult to accept that their child has any kind of additional needs based on evidence from observations. ECE students may find that they are sympathetic with the parent. ECE students must be careful not to label children, which can arise from observations. Parents can feel angry that their child is not perceived as progressing normally – whatever that means.

Other strong influences may have been imported and these can also challenge ECE students' relationship with parents. Sometimes parents can feel disempowered by the school or setting and the teaching culture, that the ethos is professionalised – almost scientific – and home learning is not valued. This can be exacerbated by parents or carers having English, or the primary language used in the setting, as their second or third language. So, parents who want the best for their children want to follow the official path, which means it is a tangible success when parents can tick off that their three-year-old child has 'coloured in' and held the crayon with the correct grip. This is the opposite of what we want to see as it stifles children's drive to explore and self-regulate and affects self-motivation. Desforges and Abouchaar (2003) suggest that schools are more inclined to work with parents in supporting the school as an institution, rather than entering into a reflective and analytical dialogue with parents. As stated by Sylva et al. (2004), unless schools reach out and link with parents, the home culture's potential for learning cannot be built upon.

The success of children's development and learning is not dependent upon them being kept busy or quiet, or even the production of a model or drawing to take home. The role of the ECE student here is to invent, design, prepare and plan a range of activities and purposeful learning experiences. Added to this, students need to think carefully about individual children and everything that the child does. What is the child's learning need? What is their stage of development? Students will need to consider this in their own right and as part of a group or class. What areas do they need additional support in? Although it is very hard to plan for all of these things, it is what the observant student tries to do in keeping observations child-focused. When students have good relationships with parents, they do not need to show them everything that their child has made, written or created. Instead, ECE students can talk to parents at length about their child, recalling whole episodes of the child's play that illustrates their learning and the process that they are going through as they learn. The challenge for ECE students is to help parents see that what we share with them is evidence of their children's powerful learning.

Debates about how best to work with parents have been ongoing since the publication of the *Plowden Report* in 1967 and the *Warnock Report* in 1978. More recent decades, however, have witnessed a change in the attitude of researchers working in this area. As pointed out by Athey (1990: 20), 'Most research in the 1960s and 1970s was designed to assist the inadequate parent.' Pugh and De'Ath (1989), Desforges and Abouchaar (2003),

Draper and Duffy (2006) and Whalley and the Pen Green Team (2001–2004) all subscribe to the same line of thinking in their assertion that all parents are interested in the development and progress of their own children.

Siraj-Blatchford et al. argue that:

> The partnership between parents and educational workers has been described by MacNaughton (2003) in terms of a conforming relationship in which educators are the professional experts on how young children learn and therefore on the best ways in which children should be educated... The professional holds the power and Carpenter et al. (1996) state that the professionals used their position to make judgements and control what needed doing. Parent partnerships at this time did not represent a two-way exchange of views and parents were not expected to have much involvement in their children's education. (2007: 50)

A wide range of research studies around this issue have been reviewed by Desforges and Abouchaar (2003: 4). They conclude that what parents do at home 'has a significant and positive effect on children's achievement and adjustments, even after all other factors shaping attainment have been taken out of the equation'. Similarly, research by Sylva et al. (2004) confirms that children are put at a disadvantage if their home and school culture are disconnected, particularly when there is no overlap in the pedagogic context. So, if we accept the concept of parents as partners as a good thing – one that embraces equality, agreement and joint endeavour – it is then necessary to recognise any structural barriers that may unwittingly prevent professionals from developing effective parent partnerships within schools and settings. For these reasons, it is important that ECE students work closely with parents so that they can provide high-quality care and education.

It is interesting to note that the Froebelian approach brings out the wrongness of 21st-century neoliberalism's view of compliance, accountability and competition as a way of educating children. Instead, children are part of a community of learners – families, teachers and students working together in helpful ways that support children's learning.

When one considers the concepts of power and knowledge, the relationship between parents, professionals and institutions is complex and uneven. The various stakeholders appear to have very different but interrelated interests and time commitments invested in the child. What is also apparent, and a direct consequence of the power being weighted heavily on the side of the institution, is that the institution takes control in this relationship, as it impacts on the school's policies. Despite these structural constraints, and the varying degree of control that institutions may have in place, all the professionals who work with children have a significant amount of power in how they choose to interact, respond and engage with parents on pedagogical issues. Knowledge and power are closely linked. Gewirtz and Cribb (2009: 7) make the point that the power of the professional 'is rooted in and sustained by their access to knowledge that is socially valued'. Given the implied inequalities in the power base of this relationship, the fact that some schools may perceive parental involvement as unimportant will have a great impact on how involved parents can be in their children's learning.

According to MacNaughton (2003: 269), the real shifts in the approach towards parents occur when there is 'transformation from [the] knowledge/power relationship to promote "democratic citizenship" by inviting parents and others to form policies, manage resources and evaluate services and by devolving decisions about what and how children should learn'.

Solutions

It is clear that the main issue is about how structural barriers affect the development of individual relationships within an institution. There is a need to focus on support for parents and for the personal development of practitioners. Structural change is arguably a central component in the movement towards a fitting model of engagement, as it serves to reinforce professional practice. It therefore follows that consideration must be given to how schools and settings actively engage parents in sharing knowledge and theoretical understandings. Equally, consideration must be given to developing strategies for professional development in order to remove the barriers that block collaboration.

Whalley and Arnold (2013: 111) make the point that institutions can unintentionally make communicating with parents difficult: 'Schools sometimes have rules that prevent children from having an equal opportunity to attend, for example, an expensive uniform, which is obligatory.' Clearly, having an awareness that change may need to happen is fundamental if information and aims are to be shared with parents. Schools must therefore be conscious that the professional and the parent are connected in this partnership, and that parents need to have an active role in the sharing of an educational vision and making decisions. Freire says:

> Perceive our own ignorance and give up the idea that we are the exclusive owners of truth and knowledge. Identify with others and recognise the fact that 'naming the world' is not the task for the elite. Value the contribution of others and listen to them with humility, respecting the particular view of the world helped by different people. (1970: 71)

In this way, Freire (1970) not only urges us to find reciprocal ways of working in partnership, but also acknowledges and accepts the complexities that are inherent when collaborating.

It is vital that schools and settings are able to demonstrate good working relationships, not only for the success of their service, but, crucially, to improve the lives of children and families in their community. Whilst looking at shifting positions and the collective sharing of power, the focus must remain on the learner. However, the ethos and value base of the school or setting, in terms of how the individual growth of professionals is facilitated, cannot be dismissed. Realistically, professionals cannot be expected to let go of the traditional power-based relationship without training, funding, resources, time and space.

Professional Development

Early Years practitioners and ECE students generally receive very little training on working with parents, yet curriculum policy documentation requires them to have a wide range of skills in order to engage with parents effectively. Unarguably, working with parents is both difficult and complex. Practitioners and students therefore need to have skills in 'handling' or 'holding' parents in ways that build on their strengths rather than deskill them. For practitioners and students to work more collaboratively with parents, they need to be able to access training that complements their curriculum framework. It is a lack of quality training that presents further barriers to effective engagement. Elfer and Dearnley (2007) suggest that the available Continuing Professional Development (CPD) programme does not adequately address practitioners' emotional attachments, thus further illuminating the gap and tensions between policy and practice. There is an urgent necessity for schools and settings to audit what they are currently doing with parents, then to critically reflect on what initiatives they need to develop and what they may have to do more of.

The level of training and support offered to practitioners is also significant – this is what will actually give impetus to the much needed shift in professional practice, because it will come with the recognition that the role of the parent is integral to their children's learning. Identifying what is needed and reviewing the quality of what is being offered will help schools and settings to begin to define and measure the effectiveness of their parental programmes and initiatives.

Finally, it is essential to establish a range of ways of sharing information with parents and carers to discuss matters of child development. Recognising the personal expertise that parents or carers bring, and the passion they may have about their child, can stimulate conversations between Early Years educators and parents or carers. Parent knowledge of their children's learning will include (adapted from Louis, 2020: 27):

- Child's personality – are they shy or outgoing?
- What sort of things do the children enjoy doing at home?
- What do their children enjoy doing outside?
- How do they react when they meet new people, both adults and children?
- What is the child like when away from the parent?

- If the child is still in nappies, can they use the toilet independently, or with some support?
- How willing is the child to try things for him or herself?
- Can the child dress themselves or put on their own shoes and coat?
- How does their child ask for help, whether in a particular language, words, signs or gestures?
- What things frighten their child?
- How does their child show frustration, anger or upset?
- How does their child play with other children?
- Is their child's speech clear? Can they talk about events, past and future?
- Does their child have a particular interest, such as superheroes, wrestling or fairies?

Discussing and Sharing Observations with Parents and Colleagues

Students can strengthen their powers of observation through talking about them with parents and colleagues, to build a deeper knowledge and understanding of learning and development. When students talk with parents and colleagues about their observations, they discover useful and insightful information about them. For example, a parent shared the following observation – Raphael (2 years, 6 months) took a roll of drawing paper and rolled it onto the floor so that some of the length was revealed but the end was still rolled up into a cylinder. He said it was his bed and lay down on it with his head at the 'pillow' end where the paper was still rolled up.

ECE students will need to think about how they can incorporate Raphael's interest into the learning environment at home and in the setting. What resources and materials would you need to support Raphael's symbolic play? Are there story books about transforming shapes that you could use? Taking a holistic look at Raphael, what aspects of his development could you further support based on the observations? It is vital that students reflect on how they plan to support children's development and learning. This is how ECE students can show parents that their knowledge is based on their observations of what the child can do and is capable of achieving.

Another parent shared this observation – after his mother read him the Russian fairy tale about Baba Yaga the witch who lived in a house on chicken legs, John (5 years 3 months) demanded to hear this story several more times. John then found another version in the library. In a drawing he blended together details from the separate stories and seemed quite happy to accept the variations. John's mum described how he talked to himself about the stories the whole time he was drawing; at no time was this drawing anything but a process. John was not at all interested in the drawing once he'd finished and looked a bit blank when asked to talk about it. John's mum found this drawing interesting because this was the first time that she had observed and understood the process of John's learning. When his mum looked more closely at the drawing she could see the house on chicken legs, Baba Yaga on her pestle and mortar (no broomsticks for Russian witches), a bone and skull fence round the house, a black bagel, and children trapped in the house. This is an interesting observation because John is taking the external stimuli of the stories into his thinking and then making his thoughts visible. It is a form of thinking.

When sharing observations with parents, ECE students can link it to Bruce's definition of teaching – 'observe, support, extend'. That way, all observations should aim to make the child's inner thinking visible. Remember that it is a privilege to observe and to listen to a child to find out how they are thinking and making sense of the world. ECE students come away understanding a bit more about the child that they are observing.

In another example, a parent shared a photograph of a nativity scene that Jada had made. There was a family crib scene, made from her set of Numicons. Jada had a little Playmobil nativity at home – this showed an amazing use of symbols from something that is symbolic itself.

Ava did some mark making showing straight and curved lines. She explained that it was snakes and ladders, which she had never played. When her dad was reading her a Shirley Hughes story, one of the illustrations showed a snakes and ladders board game which she studied very closely and asked lots of questions about. This was a really important exchange as the parent was feeling fascinated by their child's learning.

Principles of Working with Parents

- Early Years educators must have a good knowledge of the local community and amenities available to them
- Families should be involved wherever possible in the life of the setting
- Parents should be greeted by name, using the correct pronunciation, and staff should have some knowledge of where to find information for parents with a second language
- Early Years educators must recognise that parents play a vital role in their children's development and learning
- All of the resources used should reflect the different types of families attending the school or setting
- The learning experiences on offer are always culturally relevant and specific to the children's home culture and first-hand experiences
- The first point of contact should always be the key adult and communication systems should be put in place that allow for a two-way flow of information between parents and Early Years educators, particularly at the start and end of each day
- There should always be regular opportunities, both formal and informal, for parents to talk to Early Years educators about their children's learning

- All Early Years educators should commit to attending CPD training in equality and diversity
- Monthly team meetings are used to critically reflect upon the values and beliefs that underpin professional practice
- All Early Years educators should be consistently welcoming and approachable to children and their families
- Early Years educators should provide regular workshops which support parents to develop the confidence to be more involved in their children's learning and to facilitate workshops on how to support and promote children's development and learning.

(Adapted from Louis, 2020: 26).

Reflection

It is essential that students reflect on the factors that can help them to build meaningful partnerships with parents.

- How do you show that you value the knowledge that parents have about their children's development and learning?
- How would you involve parents in their child's education?
- What sort of activities would you provide to promote partnership working?
- How seriously do you take on board parents' concerns?

Conclusion

Now that we are at a stage where most Early Years schools and settings recognise the importance of having good partnerships with parents, the challenge is to find ways that are not uniform in design or regulated in approach for professionals and parents to engage in a meaningful dialogue. At one end of the spectrum is an image of good partnerships, through which professionals can enhance parental partnerships and develop, challenge and redefine methods of engagement. At the other end of the spectrum, however, is a picture of a static relationship. It therefore follows that huge leaps to acknowledge and adopt a more progressive partnership – one that reflects a more pivotal dimension and recognises when to shift in position and how to redistribute power – are much needed.

References

Athey, C. (1990) *Extending Thoughts in Young Children: A Parent-Teacher Partnership.* London: Paul Chapman.

Desforges, C. and Abouchaar, A. (2003) *The Impact of Parental Involvement, Parental Support and Family Education on Pupil Achievements and Adjustment: A Literature Review*. Research Report 433. London: DfES.

Draper, L. and Duffy, B. (2006) 'Working with parents' in G. Pugh (ed.), *Contemporary Issues in the Early Years* (4th edn). London: Sage. pp. 151–62.

Elfer, P. and Dearnley, K. (2007) 'Nurseries and emotional well-being: Evaluating an emotionally containing model of professional development'. *Early Years*, 27(3): 267–79.

Freire, P. (1970) *Pedagogy of the Oppressed*. New York: Continuum.

Gewirtz, S. and Cribb, A. (2009) *Understanding Education: A Sociological Perspective*. Cambridge: Polity Press.

Louis, S. (2020) 'Close to home'. *Nursery World*: 6–7.

MacLeod-Brudenell, I. (2004) *Advanced Early Years Care and Education*. Oxford: Heinemann.

MacNaughton, G. (2003) *Shaping Early Childhood*. Maidenhead: Open University Press.

Melhuish, E. (2007) 'The Role of Research in the Development of Sure Start'. Institute of Education. University of London 5–8 September 2007. Conference Session Number 6.12. Symposium 8719.

Miller, L., Cable, C. and Devereux, J. (2004) *Developing Early Years Practice*. London: David Fulton.

Pugh, G. and De'Ath, E. (1989) *Working Towards Partnership in the Early Years*. London: National Children's Bureau, London.

Siraj-Blatchford, I., Clarke, K. and Needham, M. (eds) (2007) *The Team Around the Child: Multi-Agency Working in the Early Years*. Stoke-on-Trent: Trentham.

Sylva, K., Melhuish, E., Sammons, P., Siraj-Blatchford, I. and Taggart, B. (2004) *The Effective Provision of Pre-School Education (EPPE) Project. Final Report: A Longitudinal Study Funded by the DfES 1997–2004*. London: Institute of Education, University of London/Department of Education and Skills/Sure Start.

Vygotsky, L.S. (1978) *Mind in Society: The Development of Higher Psychological Processes*. Cambridge, MA: Harvard University Press.

Wheeler, H. and Connor, J. (2009) 'Parents, Early and Learning: Parents as partners in the Early Years Foundation Stage – Principles into practice.' Jessica Kingsley Publishers.

Whalley, M. and Arnold, C. (2013) *Working with Families in Children's Centres and Early Years Settings*. London: Hodder Education.

Whalley, M. and the Pen Green Team (2001) *Involving Parents in their Children's Learning*. London: Paul Chapman Publishing.

10
TRANSLATING PROFESSIONAL KNOWLEDGE INTO PRACTICE

Introduction

This chapter examines the relationship between knowledge, learning and pedagogy in Early Years practice and explores the interplay between knowledge and experience using case study examples. It will also look at the complexities that lie within the creation and use of professional knowledge for students in practice, while unpicking what constitutes skilful observational practice and how observation skills evolve. More specifically, this chapter examines the student's ability to transpose this professional knowledge from theory into daily routines and observational practices. It will also explore what role Continuing Professional Development (CPD) can play in encouraging further improvement of observational methods.

Pedagogy in Practice

Observations of children's learning should, in practice, guide ECE students to facilitate and enhance development and learning in babies and young children. Students' interpretations and assessments in planning for and responding to children's individual needs are an important part of this, as is having opportunities for reflection and discussions that allow students to both refine and develop their professional knowledge and skills.

Pedagogical knowledge is about two things – knowing the content of the curriculum and how to facilitate young children's development and learning, and the ability to effectively plan and implement developmentally motivating and challenging learning experiences which seek to support or enhance the child's actual development. This involves being an observer, but also interacting – sometimes playing alongside the child to support and extend what they are interested in and being able to organise the learning environment so that children can choose what they want to do.

Defining Knowledge

Though they come from different angles, several theorists illuminate the issue of professional knowledge. These are Eraut (1994), Goodson (2003), Hargreaves (1998), Hegarty (2000), Hiebert, Gallimore and Stigler (2002) and Verloop, Van Driel and Meijer (2001). Their theories and frameworks on how practitioners contribute to learning – and the complexities inherent in their professional development – all assume similar positions. They seek to identify the relationship between different types of knowledge and the individual and make this explicit. They also agree that knowledge is fluid and constantly changing and developing, while highlighting the effect that practitioner knowledge has on learning. Eraut (2000), Hiebert et al. (2002) and Verloop et al. (2001) shed further light on this by giving consideration to the importance of a contextual and historical understanding of professional knowledge when incorporating policy implementation.

Drawing on Karl Popper's (1972) Three Worlds of Knowledge, Hiebert et al. (2002: 7) attempt to define knowledge as a concept. According to this model, knowledge is said to have three dimensions: 'World 1 – knowledge of physical and real-world objects and experiences; World 2 – individuals' knowledge and skills; and World 3 – shared ideas treatable as public objects that can be stored and accumulated.' The authors argue that most practitioners can be placed in Worlds 1 and 2. However, they assert that building sustainable professional knowledge requires practitioners to interact with Worlds 1 and 2, but also live in World 3. It is important to note that personal motivation, openness and willingness to learn varies. This will also determine an individual's readiness to access World 3.

In their effort to effectively close the gap between knowledge and practice, Hiebert et al. (2002) argue that a practitioner's knowledge is often compartmentalised into pedagogical knowledge and craft knowledge that may be separate from context. They make a clear distinction between craft and professional knowledge, suggesting that craft knowledge is rooted in a specific context that is personal, belonging only to the individual, while arguing that professional knowledge should be sharable (and actually shared) to improve and develop a practitioner's subject knowledge. They therefore recognise that knowledge must be testable and tested as a means of expert reflection. It is this verification that will connect theory to practice. Sharing ideas about teaching and learning shapes and develops an individual's experiences. As this is done, craft knowledge can be generated collaboratively and integrated into the production of a knowledge base that is public and sharable.

Observation

A nursery owner/manager, expecting an imminent inspection visit, asked a trainer to carry out some bespoke training on observation, assessment and planning for her team of eight staff. It was felt that the setting's practitioners needed to examine their observations more closely to ensure that they were objective and that they were identifying any other issues that they perceived in their children. The trainer started by asking the participants to share their interpretations of their observations with colleagues, focusing on the child's learning. The trainer set about facilitating a discussion with the ECE practitioners. This was an important starting point, as it sought to draw on practitioner knowledge.

Personal Knowledge

Eraut (2002: 114) defines personal knowledge as the 'cognitive resource that a person brings to a situation that enables them to think and perform'. It also covers the aspect of propositional knowledge, which is when a student has specific knowledge of what they are expected to do in carrying out observations, is able to describe the process, but does not know how to do it. Eraut focuses on the importance of how blended forms of knowledge inform skilled practitioners, who are able to use them precisely in fluid professional settings. He insists that 'learning is defined as the process whereby knowledge is acquired. It also occurs when existing knowledge is used in a new context or in new combinations: since this also involves the creation of new personal knowledge, the transfer process remains within this definition of learning' (Eraut, 2000: 114).

Therefore, in essence, his view is that the process of learning and not the end product is the chief factor, as is the context in which learning processes take place. He further adds the point that educators tap into their historical body of knowledge and experiences, making their tacit understandings and ways of knowing clearer. This was definitely the case in the trainer's discussions about planning and identifying particular gaps in children's learning, becoming aware of areas of difficulty and possible reasons for a child's lack of progress. The practitioners came up with a number of interventions that they could take to address a child's lack of progress.

It is important to recognise that students also provide personal care and education to children when they interpret and assess their needs and plan a range of activities to promote development. Indeed, the process of observing is both personal and professional and includes identifying and responding to babies' and young children's needs, articulating learning, developing the learning environment both indoors and outdoors in response to observations, and participating in reflective practice. It is necessary for ECE students to reflect on their ideas about pedagogy and practice in relation to professional knowledge, values and beliefs about how babies, toddlers and young children learn, and consider what this looks like in actual practice. What students believe about children has an impact on both planning and pedagogy.

Verloop et al. (2001: 443) advance the idea that a practitioner's personal knowledge is relevant and should be included with formal propositional knowledge – 'The personal knowledge of a teacher is highly determined and "coloured" by his or her individual experiences, personal history (including learning processes), personality variables, sub-ject-matter knowledge and so on.' They assert that 'personal knowledge' is what guides a practitioner's actions. What practitioners believe about the children as learners has a huge impact on both their pedagogy and their ability to plan effectively for them. The suggestion here is that knowledge comes in different forms. Therefore, we must also look out for factors that can be reconstituted when we begin to tease them out, as well as any that we may not be able to translate. By placing a greater importance on context, and the fact that ECE students need to know more about how young children actually learn cognitively, the policy trajectory can be taken forward. In the context of professional knowledge, what else could be of greater importance than the practitioner, the child, and how practitioners take on ideas that inform their interactions with children?

Subject Knowledge

It is necessary to explore what is embedded and uncover where it comes from. References to Shulman (1986) and Hegarty (2000) are useful here as they both recognise essential factors that help to determine how a practitioner's subject/content knowledge can be identified and further developed. However, Hegarty (2000) does state that the over-classi-fication of a practitioner's subject/content knowledge into the different types in use does not effectively explain how it has an impact on children's behaviour, nor does it support any real understanding of effective teaching. He goes on to say that a practitioner's sub-ject/content knowledge is actually located within the act of teaching that is informed by observation. Similarly, Shulman (1986) makes a distinction between three types of knowledge forms: propositional knowledge, which is linked to theory; case knowledge, linked to experience and encounters; and strategic knowledge, which is connected to how practitioners act when they teach. He also argues that practitioner subject/content knowl-edge can be most effectively understood in the context of teaching. Shulman's (1986) encounters and strategic knowledge is therefore parallel to that suggested by Hegarty (2000). Eraut (2000: 120) also contributes to the debate by asserting that what is needed is to provide a defensible account, rather than a description, of professionals' actions, and to create an impression of professional control over situations which inspire confidence in them as a person'. What a practitioner knows about the cognitive process of learning is at the heart of teaching. However, a practitioner's personal history must also be consid-ered, so that their aspirations, values and beliefs about early childhood and education, in relation to where they are coming from, can be located correctly.

Continuing Professional Development

In recent years, ECE students in England, Scotland and Wales have seen the introduction of new curriculum frameworks. The requirements therein put forward a universal set of principles that all ECE students working with babies and young children are expected to adhere to. Underlying the rationale of the curriculum documentation is a wealth of theoretical knowledge and research findings that are brought to the fore through publicly shared examples of observations, references and resources. All of the policy documents place great emphasis on being a professional and propose that professional knowledge is an essential ingredient. These are regulated by different bodies which serve as a means of standardising the level of professionalism within the sector.

The relationship between professional knowledge, pedagogy and practice should not be underestimated. In reality, this means keeping professional knowledge updated so that students can continue to reflect on young children's development and the curriculum framework to inform judgements and decision making in practice. It is essential that ECE students are able to draw on professional knowledge in order to promote children's learning. This is echoed by *Realising the Ambition* (Scottish Government, 2020: 10), which states: 'Continuous professional learning (CPL) is an essential component of ELC [Early Learning and Childcare] quality and is linked to children's development.' Similarly, the *Early Years Foundation Stage* (Department for Education, 2021: 26) says: 'Providers must support staff to undertake appropriate training and professional development opportunities to ensure they offer quality learning and development experiences for children that continually improve.' This suggests that they recognise CPD training as integral to effective teaching and learning. When ECE students have regular opportunities through training to update knowledge and understanding of child development, this will lead to a firmer foundation upon which they can further develop their observational skills and professional knowledge and practice.

Reflection and Knowledge

Froebel is clear that observation without reflection is an empty observation and could never lead to real understanding. Froebel, in Liebschner (1992: 141), states that, 'Previous knowledge will of course help to direct our thinking, but unless we make use of our ability to probe into the dark, unless we foster the hunch and pay attention to our presentiments, human progress would be stunted.'

ECE students can pay careful attention to their observations through the act of reflection – purposefully and deliberately returning to a significant observational experience to extract, explore and deepen learning which has been presented by it. Reflection encourages and stimulates deep learning that leads to professional development and improvement of practice. It is therefore vital that ECE students reflect on their observations for the following reasons.

- To make sense of and analyse children's actions and behaviours
- To examine your own interactions and responses
- To reflect upon assessment judgement
- To put your learning into practice through planning, interacting and resourcing
- To improve and develop your skill as an active observer
- To help you to recognise gaps in your own knowledge

Aistear, the Irish Early Childhood Curriculum Framework, states:

> The reflective adult uses information about children's learning and development to think about his/her practice, and to identify how to improve it. He/she may do this in partnership with colleagues and/or other professionals. This reflection may result in the adult changing the way he/she interacts with children and their parents, reorganising the room, changing routines, planning particular activities, and providing specific materials and objects. The adult also shares assessment information with the children and their parents and uses the information to plan for children's progress. (2009: 71)

Reflection involves slowing down and taking time out of your busy day to look more closely at your observations and inquire about them. It is essential that ECE students recognise that the process of reflection will enable them to better understand their observations and interpretations, thereby extending their thinking. It can also help to develop and improve practice by identifying, through the sharing of observations, what students need to know in order to advance understanding about the child's development and learning. It also helps students to bring together all observational data in order to make sense of feedback and new observations from others.

This is reinforced by Boud, Keogh and Walker:

> Reflection is an important human activity in which people recapture their experience, think about it, mull it over and evaluate it. It is this working with experience that is important in learning. The capacity to reflect is developed to different stages in different people and it may well be those abilities which characterise those who learn effectively from experience. (1985: 19)

Practitioner Comments

ECE students will need to recognise that it is not good enough to just observe without thinking about the links, complexities, patterns and connections in the child's play and explorations. Thinking and linking enables practitioners to learn. Returning back to the trainer in the setting, pedagogical knowledge was shared between the practitioners in regard to the learning environment, which they then organised together in response to their observations. They discussed their key children's interests and ensured that all of the children had activities and experiences that would motivate them to investigate, enquire, explore and be curious. From their discussions it became clear how interrelated personal and professional knowledge is with their experience. It is clear that developing a knowledge base for practitioners is not as simple as the three characteristics asserted by Hiebert et al. (2002). Some of the comments from practitioners who took part in the discussions included:

> 'It allowed me to reflect and think about my feeling about the child more and reflect on my own bias to stereotype children by gender and ethnicity in my observations.'

> 'Had we not discussed our observations I don't think I would have considered the importance of talking about and reflecting on my interpretations with the others for my own development.'

> 'I found the discussions about the observations that we had gathered extremely helpful when planning. It enabled me to think more deeply and consciously about my key child's previous learning and what was happening and why I needed to make his learning meaningful.'

Developing Professional Knowledge

Hiebert et al. (2002: 6) go further by putting forward the notion that a 'consequence of generating knowledge linked with practice is that it is detailed, concrete and specific'. The practitioners in the case study certainly found this to be the case – as the trainer shared knowledge with them, by outlining examples about their actual practice rather than the abstract notions of observe, assess and plan, the trainer was able to engage the practitioners in developing a knowledge base that directly linked with and made connections to their everyday practice.

Eraut (1994: 31) continues by recognising a significant link between context and practitioner learning. He argues that educators are more immersed in the 'doing environment' than the 'knowing environment'. He suggests that this creates a reliance on a 'procedural knowledge' that is often acquired unreflectively, dictating that knowledge is merely obtained and too heavily based on theory – with rules, ideas, techniques and principles of theories totally guiding professional practice. He promotes the idea that systems need to be able to capture knowledge and specifically see the interdependence of the interplay between blended knowledge forms. Adding more detail, he describes his concept of 'relevant knowledge' as being a knowledge that is ready for use and constructed from personal experience, reflection, social interaction, acculturation, skills and practice. This is particularly important when considering how knowledge is transferred between different contexts. Knowing precisely what kind of knowledge is needed when making decisions or dealing with new situations in teaching requires an ability to recognise the different types of knowledge relevant to new situations. According to Eraut, in order for educators to integrate the different aspects of knowledge, they must learn how to locate and pull relevant knowledge out of previous situations and contexts. It is through this interplay that knowledge is transformed. In the case study, one of the practitioners took part in this interplay for the first time, taking responsibility for monitoring and evaluating progress of her key child, including liaising with any other specialist who delivered support.

In a similar vein, Hiebert et al. (2002: 6) suggest, 'Practitioner knowledge is useful for practice precisely because it develops in response to specific problems in practice.' They elaborate on this by saying that professionals need a knowledge base that is fluid in the way in which it links theory to practice, showing this fluidity in its ability to grow and be subsequently improved. The authors put forward another key element of what a professional knowledge base should look like – that it is crucial for practitioners to be able to share and evaluate their practice with colleagues. They argue that, via this pathway, opportunities are created for professionals to build a knowledge base that is actually sustainable for their professional requirements. This dimension brings critical and important issues about what 'relevant knowledge' is to the surface. The practitioners took part in regular group discussions, sharing their observations.

Learning in Practice

The issue of sharing observations raises two questions. First, are practitioners accessing professional knowledge appropriately? Second, when this knowledge has been gained, is it being transposed into action to create a learning ethos where students want to develop further? These constitute the missing link between theory and practice at a very fundamental level and this gap must be bridged if students are to independently incorporate their professional knowledge and personal experiences into their practice.

Eraut (1994: 20) draws attention to how practitioners learn in the workplace. He explores the importance of experience in generating new knowledge, arguing that 'professional knowledge is constructed through experience and its nature depends on cumulative acquisition, selection and interpretation of that experience'. To complement this, the usefulness of Hiebert et al.'s (2002) 'consequences' of formulating new knowledge and understanding can be seen to support a crossover of information as theory is translated into practice.

Towards Understanding the Personal in the Professional

The case study highlights how the use of concrete examples greatly aided the process. The trainer found that these pre-school practitioners showed great interest once the question of 'repeated actions' made by their children was brought up. This triggered an in-depth discussion initiated by the manager about how children learn. As a concrete example, this supported the practitioners' efforts to begin to understand and make connections with the mostly normal reference criteria of the policy documentation – in particular, that children learn through play and exploration. It also presented learning as a process and not merely an end product, focused on the need for the practitioners to understand and become familiar with this criteria before imposing their own interpretations on the play and exploration observed. As a result of this breakthrough, the manager, and indeed the practitioners, began to show a much-improved understanding of child development. This is significant – through changing their own personal attitude, the manager was better placed to develop and change the attitude of the practitioners.

All of the curriculum policy documentation featured in this book promotes pedagogy as an important feature of professional knowledge. Shulman (1986) and Hiebert et al. (2002) insist that teaching requires a complex integration of pedagogical knowledge, subject knowledge and knowledge about how children learn. ECE students must therefore have a comprehensive pedagogical knowledge and understanding that can be applied to all areas of learning as described in Chapter 9. The real significance lies in how the leadership team supports the translation of knowledge from function, context and content into practice. It is these aspects of Early Years leadership and management that require a deep conceptual understanding of child development. Consequently, it also follows that precise recognition of what pedagogical knowledge is, and how it can best be shared as a means of developing practitioners and influencing others, has implications not only for practitioners, but also for managers and leaders. This is because pedagogical knowledge is critical to improving understanding of how children learn. Quality of leadership is therefore critical to supporting Early Years practitioners and ECE students in the work that they do and is central to initiating and sustaining the individual's professional development. The policy documentation provides a sound insight into child development, but it still needs to be fine-tuned on issues relating to leadership – there needs to be much more thought and discussion among policymakers about integrating aspects of the leaders knowledge to improve and develop practice in the required contexts.

Knowledge in Practice

As the training continued, the pre-school practitioners became keen to familiarise themselves with observable stages of children's drawings, thereby integrating relevant public and personal knowledge into their new understanding as they practised their pedagogical role (Eraut, 1994). They began to see how much one act could transform their previous understandings, capturing the interdependence and interplay between knowledge acquisition and the learning process. By the end, these pre-school practitioners were clear that the role they play in supporting learning is fundamental and crucial. This development shows the relevance of Eraut's (2000: 126) and Goodson's (2003: 67) assertions that a practitioner's 'knowledge is highly personal'.

The particular emphasis on knowledge being highly personal is central to the pre-school practitioners' training experience as they made frequent references to their personal impressions of teaching and learning and its cultural construction. From this perspective, a useful definition of culture is that it is a whole range of values, customs and social institutions that distinguish the way of life for a particular community. Banks et al. (1999) add to this, suggesting that knowledge construction is shaped by cultural identification and the interpretation of educational content. How students interpret, integrate and transform aspects of knowledge has major implications for their personal sense of being a professional. This was seen in an example where one of the practitioners had considered that real learning only takes place on a formal basis (as opposed to a creative basis), supporting her stance with the suggestion that parents wanted formal learning. For the practitioner, the idea of children's self-initiated and self-chosen activities made her work more complicated.

Learning from Experience

Hiebert et al. (2002) assert that practitioners need to learn from experience. This was certainly the case during the training. The trainer considered ways in which she could support the practitioners to apply their existing knowledge to a new situation leading to further knowledge, with the practitioners beginning to look beyond the surface of their observations. Kolb (1984) talks about the 'experiential learning cycle' as practise, reflect, interpret and plan. Kolb emphasises that going through and following up each stage in the cycle is of equal importance, stating (1984: 38), 'Learning is the process whereby knowledge is created through the transformation of experience.' Throughout their interactions, the participants did indeed begin to make connections and show that they were better able to value the children's 'free time' as an opportunity for them to observe their individual interests, without imposing their culturally defined train of thought or actions. It was in this context that the practitioners experienced the value of being a reflective professional (Schon, 1983; Bolton, 2005; Dymoke and Harrison, 2008; Pollard et al., 2008). Ultimately, it was their own immediate willingness to change tack and tune into their knowledge and implicit theories when faced by their indifference that created the impetus which led to this responsiveness to the trainer's methods. Much of the individual learning took place during the different stages of the process.

As has been suggested by Eraut (2000), the trainer became acutely aware and was able to facilitate a process of knowledge transfer – the practitioners used the training to inform their practice, becoming more skilled in it and developing a greater appreciation of it. Subsequently, because of their ultimate readiness to learn through a new process, the preschool was later graded 'good' in the inspection.

Developing Professional Practice

How practitioners acquire professional knowledge to develop children's learning involves a number of enhancements to professional practice – these include increased ability in guiding professional practice; looking more closely at how practitioners transpose theory into practice and the ability to share, facilitate and further develop themselves and individuals; and developing professional practice. Many of these benefits draw upon the individual practitioners' strengths and skills in how they develop their own knowledge. Certainly, all professionals need to contextualise, use and re-use their ideas in order to refresh their professional knowledge and practice. Eraut (2000: 130) states that 'knowledge is shaped by context(s) in which it is acquired and used'. It is important to recognise that the above enhancements might only hold good when they relate to concrete and specific individual training and development needs. It is acknowledged that learning is indeed a complex process that incorporates a historic body of knowledge for the learner and includes experiences that are both social and individual. Three points need to be made – these relate to the capacity of practitioners to develop professional practice, their personal motivation, and knowledge transfer.

Reflection

- How are you using your professional knowledge in your observations?
- What personal and professional development could you undertake to support and improve your observations?
- What literacy or numeracy strategy do you use?
- Can you describe how you plan, organise and sequence individual children's learning?
- How frequently do you monitor the effectiveness of your learning environment?

Conclusion

It is arguable that individual learning processes and personal motivation are linked to the development and sustenance of professional knowledge. From this viewpoint, a practitioner's knowledge is linked to practice and, indeed, is motivated by the problems of practice. In addition, professional knowledge is connected to the process of learning – as put forward by Hiebert et al. (2002), it is this process that actually impacts on a practitioner's practice and knowledge base. The significance of the knowledge transfer process, both for the trainer and the practitioners, should not be taken too lightly – all of them experienced a connection when they shared and reflected on their observations, receiving helpful feedback and suggestions from others. There was evidence of some attitudinal change in one of the practitioners concerning perceptions of gender and race. It is this process that facilitates exactly how ECE practitioners acquire the 'relevant knowledge' necessary to develop not only themselves, but also, essentially, children's development and learning.

References

Banks, F., Leach, J. and Moon, B. (1999) 'New understandings of teachers' pedagogic knowledge' in J. Leach and B. Moon (eds), *Learners and Pedagogy*. London: Paul Chapman.

Bolton, C. (2005) *Reflective Practice* (2nd edn). London: Sage.

Boud, D., Keogh, R. and Walker, D. (1985) *Promoting Reflection in Learning: A Model. Reflection: Turning Reflection into Learning*. London: Routledge.

Department for Education (2021) *Statutory Framework for the Early Years Foundation Stage*.

Dymoke, S. and Harrison, J. (eds) (2008) *Reflective Teaching & Learning*. London: Sage.

Eraut, M. (1994) *Developing Professional Knowledge and Competence*. London: Falmer Press.

Eraut, M. (2000) 'Non-formal learning and tacit knowledge in professional work'. *British Journal of Educational Psychology*, 70(1): 113–36.

Eraut, M. (2002) 'Conceptual Analysis and Research Questions: Do the Concepts of "Learning Community" and "Community of Practice" Provide Added Value?'. *AERA Conference Paper*, New Orleans, April 2002.

Goodson, I.F. (2003) *Professional Knowledge, Professional Lives*. Maidenhead: Open University Press/McGraw Hill Education.

Hargreaves, A. (1998) 'The emotional practice of teaching'. *Teaching and Teacher Education*, 14(8): 835–54.

Hegarty, S. (2000) 'Teaching as a knowledge-based activity'. *Oxford Review of Education*, (26)3/4: 451–65.

Hiebert, J., Gallimore, R. and Stigler, J. (2002) 'A knowledge-base for the teaching profession: What would it look like and how can we get one?' *Educational Researcher*, 31(5): 3–15.

Kolb, D.A. (1984) *Experiential Learning: Experience as the Source of Learning and Development*. Englewood Cliffs, N.J.: Prentice-Hall.

Liebschner, J. (1992) *A Child's Work: Freedom and Guidance in Froebel's Educational Theory and Practice*. Cambridge: Lutterworth.

National Council for Curriculum and Assessment (NCCA) (2009) *Aistear: The Early Childhood Curriculum Framework*. Dublin: National Council for Curriculum and Assessment.

Popper, K.R. (1972) *Objective Knowledge*. Oxford: Clarendon Press.

Pollard, A.J., Maddock, M., Swaffield, S., Warin, J. and Warwick, P. (2008) *Reflective Teaching* (3rd edn). London: Continuum.

Schon, D.A. (1983) *The Reflective Practitioner: How Professionals Think in Action*. New York: Basic Books.

The Scottish Government (2020) *Realising the Ambition: National Practice Guidance for Early Years in Scotland*. Edinburgh: The Scottish Government.

Shulman, L.S. (1986) 'Those who understand: Knowledge growth in teaching'. *Educational Researcher*, (15)2: 4–14.

Verloop, N., Van Driel, J. and Meijer, P. (2001) 'Teacher knowledge and the knowledge-base of teaching'. *International Journal of Educational Research*, (35)5: 441–81.

INDEX